"Spare, elegant writing traces a daughter's search for the truth about her father's suicide and a psychological journey back to a WWII death camp ... a revelatory and compelling memoir."

—**Lee Smith**, author of *Blue Marlin*

"Mirinda Kossoff's father was a shape-shifter, a Jewish-turned-Southern Baptist dentist-pilot-farmer who never managed to escape the stigma of otherness or the pain of unbelonging. In this memoir, full of heart and heartbreak, Kossoff reflects on her father's legacy and her own journey of self-invention and reinvention. A frank, moving, timely story."

—**Kim Church**, author of *Byrd*

"*The Rope of Life* is a deep account of an issue we all struggle with: Identity. Born to a Baptist mother and a man who converted from Judaism, Kossoff watched her father take on roles that served him and roles that he fought against.

As he acted out in anger at times, she began to wonder if he had left an essential part of himself behind somewhere. Kossoff writes deftly about how one man's severed identity affected another generation. Moving and beautiful, *The Rope of Life* reaches a poignant conclusion. You won't regret reading this one."

—**Nancy Peacock**, author of *The Life and Times of Persimmon Wilson*

# The Rope of Life

*a memoir*

## Mirinda Kossoff

**LYSTRA BOOKS**
& Literary Services

The Rope of Life: A Memoir
Copyright © 2020 by Mirinda Kossoff
All rights reserved.

ISBN paperback: 978-1-7336816-7-4
ISBN ebook: 978-1-7336816-81-
Library of Congress Control Number: 2020911561

All family photographs are from the Kossoff family archives.

Author's photograph by Vic Benedict

Front cover photo editing by Barbara Tyroler

Book design by Kelly Prelipp Lojk

Publisher, Lystra Books & Literary Services, LLC,
391 Lystra Estates Drive, Chapel Hill, NC 27517
lystrabooks@gmail.com

❧❧❧❧❧

*To all who suffer from the pain
of being excluded and marginalized
through intolerance in all its forms.*

❧❧❧❧❧

# A NOTE TO READERS

I wrote this memoir from the heart and soul of the girl I once was, through the lens of the woman I have become. Though memories can be slippery things, I have interrogated my memories in order to write as truthfully as possible about the people and episodes in my life. I have verified dates and events that relate to historic material. My goal has been to understand, not to indict. To protect their privacy, I have changed the names of some of the people in my book, including the names of my three younger siblings. I did so because my siblings expressed the desire not to be involved. While I wanted to honor their wishes with absolute silence, I found it impossible to write my story without them being at least a small part of it. They know and have agreed to the minor part they play in the book, as well as their pseudonyms.

# ❧❧❧❧ PROLOGUE ❧❧❧❧

On one of my weekend visits home, Dad asked if I wanted to go up in his Cessna with him. Despite my concerns about his health and his ability to fly the plane, I agreed. I didn't want to disappoint him, nor did I want him to think I'd lost confidence in him.

Dad had flown in World War II, and his wartime memories must have figured large in his renewing his pilot's license at age fifty. The Cessna 172 Skyhawk wasn't simply a quick way for Dad to get to the Outer Banks for fishing weekends. The Cessna was youth, adventure, camaraderie, and risking life in the service of an ideal.

My brother Roger, brother-in-law Kip, and I were the only ones in the family crazy enough to fly with him, and I succumbed only once. We took off from the strip behind the house near Danville for a fly-over of Smith Mountain Lake, about sixty miles away, and our cottage, with its dock and covered port for the motorboat.

As Dad eased the Cessna into the sky and we gained altitude, I saw the tops of the pine trees surrounding our house and felt the plane shudder as it hit air currents higher up.

"Geez, Dad," I said. "I've never been in a plane this small. It feels like we're puppets on a string being dangled by some giant hand."

"Yup, it's great, isn't it?" Dad replied, looking left and down from his window. "But I'm the one who's in control." As he said this, I noticed he was sweating.

I was not reassured, but I kept this feeling to myself.

"I don't have a transponder in this plane yet," Dad murmured off-handedly. "So, I'll have to navigate by landmarks."

*Oh great. Now he tells me.* Then I reminded myself that Dad had flown to the Outer Banks and back several times without incident, that Roger and Kip had survived a couple of flights, so what was I worrying about?

"Well, which landmarks are we looking for?" I asked, wanting to be helpful and at the same time, wanting to be sure he was on top of it.

"We're going to fly west to Martinsville and then up 220 until I see Route 40 to Smith Mountain," Dad said.

"But how can you tell? There are so many roads down there."

"I can see the main route, and I can see Martinsville. After that, we'll follow the road north until it joins 40."

To me, the landscape below was a jumble of trees and ribbons of road. I had to believe that Dad was better at picking out landmarks than I. During the war, hadn't he found bombing targets from above?

"There it is," he said, jabbing his finger in the air below his window. I looked down and saw the ragged edge of shoreline and the sun glinting diamonds off the surface of the lake.

And below was our lakefront cottage—looking like a large Monopoly game piece—up the hill from a miniature dock.

"Remember when I learned to ski and tried to slalom with a non-slalom ski? I twisted my knee when I fell and had to be on crutches when I went back to school that fall. Remember that, Dad?"

"Yeah, sure," Dad said absently. He was focusing on the scene below. "I've lost track of 220. We're running low on gas, and I know there's a quicker way back. I'll have to find some different landmarks."

A surge of fear heated up my intestines. But I stayed mum. I didn't want to distract him, and I knew I was of no use in helping him navigate us home.

"Well, I'm not sure where we are right now." Dad chuckled. Maybe he could make light of our situation with false bravado, but it sure wasn't working for me.

"How much longer do we have on the fuel that's left?" I asked.

"We'll get there before it runs out."

"Well, that sure is a relief," I said, not meaning to be sarcastic, but fear had overcome tact.

"Ah, we're east of Martinsville. I can see 54."

He sighed and I exhaled in relief, too. Almost home. Almost safe. But then I realized we had to land.

As the Cessna's wings teetered on approach to the strip of turf behind the house, I could see Dad clench the steering wheel. He was sweating and breathing hard and seemed to have deflated, like a tire losing air. I held my breath and gripped the edges of my seat while Dad concentrated on the airstrip between the groves of pine trees below. He made one pass at the strip but then pulled up and circled around for another try. As he finally set the wheels down, we bounced like a rubber ball until the Cessna mercifully rolled to a stop, and I spilled out of the cockpit, so delirious to be back on solid ground that I wanted to kneel, like the Pope, and kiss the earth.

"Well, Dad, that was quite a ride," I said, more heartily than I was feeling.

"Next time, I'll give us a smoother landing," he said.

"Right, Dad," I replied, thinking that there wasn't going to be a next time for me. I'd proven my loyalty and once would have to be enough.

My father had always been a mystery to me, a puzzle comprising many pieces I could never put together. Even as I climbed into the Cessna with him, he was remote and unreadable. He was fifty-three years old then, not old, and I was thirty, not a child, and we were at a crossroads. Debilitating back pain had reduced him to a phantom of his former hyperactive, optimistic self. His confidence was shaky. He worked less and less. He was not the father I knew growing up, the one I looked up to as fearless, strong, funny, protective, and controlling.

After college, I fled my hometown to live in Japan, followed a few years later by nine months in England. While my world was expanding, his was shrinking. It frightened me to learn the extent to which he had withered, while I was living my life apart from his.

In his wartime photo album—the one I dragged from his closet shelf—Dad was the rakish twenty-year-old pilot who'd enlisted at nineteen. "Flying is good living," he wrote as an introduction to his collection of World War II photos. In one picture, he's dressed in his leather bomber jacket, hat with ear-flaps, flight goggles perched on his forehead. He is squatting in front of his B-17 along with his crew—other young men barely out of boyhood, with names like Augie, Bev, Fletcher, and Stoop. They're all grinning, having just survived their thirteenth bombing mission over Germany.

*Hugh Kossoff, flight goggles on his head, standing far left, in front of his B-17 with other crew members.*

*Hugh Kossoff in his Army Air Corps dress uniform.*

Dad was a top turret gunner and flight engineer. The Yank stationed in England. The cocky Jewish Yank kid with the big nose. The cocky Jewish Yank kid who saved the crew on a mission when the fuel line froze by peeing on it.

The death rate for airmen in WWII was 46 percent. I had the feeling that nothing that came later in his life could compare to the camaraderie and death-defying adventure of Dad's two years in England.

My father, named Hugo on his birth certificate, was both the bright, restless, resourceful New York Jew with a wide-open future, and Dr. Hugh Kossoff, the settled dentist and family man who married a Southern countrywoman and became a deacon in a Southern Baptist church. He was Hugo, a man with Russian roots and exposure to high culture, and Hugh, the good ol' boy in his frayed flannel shirt, a wad of tobacco tucked into his cheek, cradling a shotgun and crouching in a duck blind before dawn on a Saturday morning. He was egalitarian in a town that prided itself on social class. Social mores meant little to him, and though he seemed to want to blend in, he was at heart a nonconformist.

My father had what some would describe as a big nose. It was a long straight nose that went well with his hazel eyes, thick dark brown hair, and fleshy lips. When I was a girl, I thought he could pass for a movie star. I could see him standing in for William Holden in *The*

*Bridge Over the River Kwai* or John Kerr in *South Pacific*. He was handsome with that nose, but it gave him away. Too Jewish. Eventually, he would get a nose job, with the same intent as when he changed his name from Hugo to Hugh and his religious identity from Jewish to Southern Baptist.

And the New York accent. He got rid of that, too. Replaced it with a mild drawl—the one I grew up with. I didn't know him when he spoke like a Yankee. He wore crew cuts long after they were fashionable. He became a Republican. Back then, you could fit all the Republicans in Danville, Virginia, into a phone booth. He said he switched parties when President Truman fired General Douglas MacArthur. Being a northerner and a Republican would not have endeared him to Danville natives, most of whom were yellow-dog Democrats, meaning that they would vote for a yellow

*Sadye and Herman Kossoff with young Hugo (Hugh). Hugo was their first and only child. As he grew, he proved to be an adventurous and ingenious kid, building a sailboat that was sea-worthy and shooting off a homemade canon from his front yard in Mt. Vernon, New York.*

dog over a Republican. They weren't liberal. They were simply against the party that freed the slaves.

Dad's birth was not planned, and his parents, Sadye and Herman Kossoff, stopped sleeping in the same room after he was conceived. He was an only child who may have felt unwanted even if he didn't know the circumstances of his birth. What I know of Dad's childhood came from my mother, because Dad never talked about it. According to her—as she must have gotten it from Dad—my father, when only twelve, regularly took the train from Mount Vernon, New York, where he lived, into Manhattan and roamed the streets alone. Dad confirmed this, but he wouldn't tell me what he did on those days he explored the city, said he didn't remember.

There's a newspaper clipping handed down in the family. Dad, also at age twelve, built a small one-man sailboat with a thirteen-year-old friend named George. The boys named it *Davey Jones*, against maritime tradition. The article says the two spent a total of one dollar and thirty cents on materials and thirty hours of labor to build it. No one thought the boat would float, but the two enterprising kids took it to Long Island Sound off Fort Slocum and launched it. It proved seaworthy with only a couple of small leaks easily plugged. Unfortunately, the article doesn't mention whether Dad or George took the *Davey Jones* out on its maiden voyage.

Another true Dad-story involved his building a cannon and shooting it off from the front yard of his house. He was in his early teens at the time.

At sixteen, he ran away from home and got all the way to Florida, where he ran out of money. The story goes that a Florida man, who was a Mason, saw Dad's DeMolay ring— the DeMolays being somewhat like junior Masons—and gave him the money to take the train back to New York. This, too, Dad confirmed, but without further detail.

I was intrigued by the stories and I had a lot of questions for Dad. Try as I might, I could not engage him in a conversation about his youth, except for him to say that he enjoyed summers on Lake Taghkanic in the Hudson Valley. My grandfather and his siblings had bought cottages on the lake and gathered there in the summers. Grandpa Herman's cottage was all knotty pine and sat right on the shore. Relatives in nearby cottages could hear him playing the piano and often strolled by to listen.

I imagined Dad's summers at the lake as idyllic. Interesting cousins to play and boat and swim with. Listening to my grandfather play the piano, which I adored.

## 2

My parents met in Greensboro, North Carolina, where my father was stationed at the Overseas Replacement Depot, waiting for his assignment in World War II.

My mother, Nancy Ozelle Whitfield, was volunteering at the USO when a friend introduced her to my father. She was nine years his senior—a blue-eyed, plain-pretty woman with a large, smooth forehead and brown wavy hair. Years later, she claimed that she didn't know Dad was Jewish—or so young. My father fervently pursued her, even though she was a fundamentalist Southern Baptist who lived with her mother, Elsie Mirinda Whitfield Covington, in a Greensboro apartment. The courtship fit with his unconventional nature. Dad visited Nancy and her mother whenever he could get a pass from base. He sometimes forged the passes.

My mother's twin, Martha, was already married to Walter Corsbie. Walter was in Europe, a clerk in the US Army.

Elsie took to Hugh and in the Southern tradition of coddling the men in the family, she regularly cooked for him, plying him with Southern fried chicken, biscuits and gravy, collard greens, and every manner of over-cooked vegetable known to the South. Her homemade apple pies were a favorite, but banana pudding was the *ne plus ultra*. It was the love by food and the attention both women showered upon him that seduced the part-boy, part-man who became my father.

Though my mother never could or would say what had attracted her to my father, she must have found him exotic, exuding a whiff of the excitement she was denied growing up on a farm. He asked her to marry him before he shipped out. "No. I don't want to be a war widow," she replied.

Two years later, in September 1945, Dad was back home in New York and phoned her.

"Are you married?" he asked.

She said no.

"Engaged?"

No.

"Seeing anyone?"

No.

"Want to pick up where we left off?"

Yes.

My mother had escaped rural life near Pilot Mountain, North Carolina, to work in Greensboro as a licensed practical nurse, but the hard fact of it was that there had been few men around during the war, and my mother was nearing thirty-one. In those days, she bordered on spinsterhood. Here was a handsome, virile, younger man—a returning war hero—who wanted to marry her.

I discovered a trove of Dad's 1945 letters in the back of my mother's bureau drawer after her death in 2000. They were written during the three and a half months between my father's return to New York until he and my mother were married in December of the same year. The entire two years he was overseas, Dad never wrote my mother. Said he wanted to forget her. But he didn't forget.

Dad wrote the first letter to my mother, dated September 11, 1945.

*Dearest Nancy,*

*Well, the prodigal son returned home. Got in last week on the Queen Elizabeth, had a swell reception in NY and a swell steak dinner at Camp Kilmer with all the trimmings.*

*Not much change in me except I feel and look a lot older, 'ahem,' still free, white and 21. Got in 26 missions with the 8th Air Force and shot down an ME – 109 April 7th on our way over to bomb Gustrow, an ordnance depot. Made a couple of hauls to Berlin and had all hell shot out of us. Not much else about that except I finally made Tech Sgt.*

*We were stationed at Great Ashfield, 70 miles north of London, in "Buzz Bomb Alley," as they (the German war planes) used to come over every night.*

*Well, enough beating around the proverbial bush. Here's the straight "poop." I report for re-assignment to Greensboro on Oct. 5th. So if you answer this epistle, I will try and get there a little earlier so I can see you, though I imagine there will be plenty of passes for us while we are there.*

*Whatever happens, I won't be in the army much longer as I have 79 points and the discharge score is 80, so as soon as they lower it again, I'll be out, savvy? I figure in about three months at the most.*

*So I'll be seeing you in a few weeks my dear. Say, did you know that I'm going upstate to lease an old airplane this weekend? I've got a lot of plans for when I get out. Tell you all about them when I see you.*

*Love & Kisses – Hugh*

In another letter, before my mother was set to meet his parents, Dad suggested that she tell them she was twenty-six (instead of thirty), if asked. I got the sense, from his end of the correspondence, that my mother

*Nancy Whitfield, the author's mother, at age 29. Nancy met Hugh while volunteering at the USO during WWII. Hugh never wrote her during his two years fighting in Europe, ostensibly because she refused to marry him before he shipped out.*

was balking at meeting her future in-laws, because he tells her in his letter that it's best to be diplomatic in case they ever need his parents' help.

Dad was looking for apartments near his parents' home in Mount Vernon and in Manhattan. Herman and Sadye Kossoff were vehemently against Dad marrying a Gentile, let alone a Southern woman, let alone converting to her faith.

On November 10, Dad wrote this to my mother about his father:

> *Dad got nosey and read a couple of letters you sent me. I got mad as hell for him reading my mail and we weren't on speaking terms for a while. He says I'm crazy to get married, and I told him that he wasn't marrying you so not to worry about it and to mind his own business if he ever wanted to see me again after we were married. But don't let it worry you Darling he's cooling off already, but let's be on our guard because he's tricky at times.*
>
> *All of my Eternal Love – Hugh*

My Jewish grandparents' attempts to separate the two only hardened Dad's resolve and hurt and angered my mother, a response that would last her lifetime. They were not at the wedding when it took place on December 23, 1945, in Greensboro, at the home of my mother's half-sister, Pearl. By then, my father had converted to my mother's faith.

All of Dad's scouting for a place to live in New York came to naught, and I doubt my mother had any intention of living in New York near her in-laws. She likely persuaded Dad to settle in Greensboro, where he worked at Western Electric as an instrument technician and as a personnel officer with the NC National Guard.

Sometime after they married, the two headed west to Burbank, California, where Dad worked at Lockheed Aircraft for about a year, and then tried to launch his own business in aircraft parts. That enterprise went bust, and they returned to North Carolina, where Dad decided he would use the G.I. Bill to get an education and become a dentist.

During the time between California and North Carolina, I was conceived and born February 4, 1948, at Sternberger Hospital in Greensboro. My parents named me Mirinda for my maternal grandmother and great-grandmother, and Jean, for one of Mom's half-sisters. From early on, everyone called me Jean, except my Jewish grandparents, to whom I was Jeannie.

I was told that the nurse who brought me in to my mother said, "Thank God she doesn't have his nose."

Grandpa Herman Kossoff wrote a letter dated March 11, 1948:

*Dear Children (all three of you),*
*How is the happy little family? I trust that all of you are well and happy.*
*Jean must be quite a girl already (little Hermina). I don't believe Grandma Sadye likes the idea of Jean looking*

*like a Kossoff, especially Herman, and in all sincerity I don't blame her—after all your pappy is res adonis—yet really, I am blameless—so you'll all have to like it.*

*Well, in all seriousness now, perhaps during the Easter holidays we may come up for a day or two—as soon as I can plan my teaching schedule. I'll let you know. Of course, I suppose a weekend would be best, since Hugh will be free from work Saturday and Sunday. We are very anxious and look forward with joy to that trip to see all of you; may I say especially my little granddaughter Jean? The thought of first meeting is very exciting.*

*Enclosed you will please accept these little gifts—one for Mother Nancy and one for Baby Jean (I think a mother deserves some credit also).*

*All our love to the Kossoff trio,*
*and we shall be seeing you soon,*
*Dad*

If Grandpa Herman harbored any ill will toward my mother, his letter doesn't show it. Instead, he makes a point of sending her a gift after my birth. Could my birth have prompted a détente?

Dad entered UNC-Chapel Hill the year I was born. There I am in photos as a baby, a toddler, and finally, a three-year-old tyke with dark curly hair and bright blue eyes on a tricycle in front of our home in Victory Village. Male students with families were not allowed to live in UNC's dormitories, and there was a housing shortage for married students after the war. The birth of Victory Village—its barracks and pre-fab houses—was in response to the housing crisis. In one historical account, 352 families were living in the village when it was at capacity. Another chronicler said, "The barracks are like apartment houses with extra-thin walls. The occupants say you can hear every word from the apartments next

*The author at age 3 in front of Victory Village family housing at Univerisity of North Carolina-Chapel Hill, where Hugh used the GI Bill to get his undergraduate degree in three years.*

door. If a wife in a middle apartment calls 'honey' to her husband, she may get three responses."

My parents must have had to converse quietly, because we lived in one of those thin-walled apartments. Dad worked two jobs and Mom took in laundry and sewing to support us. Still, Dad finished his undergraduate degree in three years. He made the dean's list every semester.

In 1951, we moved to Baltimore, Maryland, where Dad earned his doctorate of dental surgery in 1954. We lived in an area called Middle River, a working-class neighborhood. My sister Mary was born there, four years after my birth, followed by my brother Roger eighteen months later.

My only memory of Middle River is of the Catholic girl who lived next door. One spring Sunday, I watched from our living room window as she glided from her house in a white gown and diaphanous veil, dancing

*Hugh and Nancy at Hugh's graduation from dental school.
The author is on the left, along with a second cousin on her
paternal side, George Wachtel.*

by the buttery daffodils that lined the sidewalk on her
way to her family's car. I begged my parents to become
Catholic so that I, too, could wear the "wedding" dress.
They said I could wear a wedding dress when I got married and not before.

When my brother was yet to be born, my mother tended my infant sister, so I had Dad all to myself at bedtime.
He read and sang to me as I lay under the quilt Grandma
Covington had made. He sat in a chair that faced the bed
so we could see each other. *The Adventures of Idabell and
Wakefield* by Betty S. Fix, a series of books that Grandpa
Herman and Grandma Sadye presented me for my fourth
birthday, was my favorite. The illustrations of the characters from those books swirled in my head forever—the
mermaid Goddess Crystal, the singing nautilus shell on
its pillow of blue velvet edged with gold, the royal fish
children—Idabell and Wakefield. The exotic life under
the sea beckoned to my pre-school self.

For most of my time living at home, I slept under that quilt Grandma Covington made for me. Its patchwork squares had no pattern but were a jumble of old fabric pieces or worn-out clothing she had saved. I studied the different patterns and colors, imagining what the scraps had been in their previous lives—a housedress, an apron, a church dress. Lying under that quilt made me feel secure, the weight of it like a warm embrace. With Dad by my side, I felt like the center of the universe.

❖❖❖❖❖

After Dad earned his DDS, the search for a practice began. My parents wanted to live in Winston-Salem, to be close to my mother's twin sister and her family. Dad took the NC dental boards and was told he, the man who graduated twentieth in a class of over one hundred, had flunked. He knew he hadn't flunked. My mother spoke to her former boss, a doctor, about why Dad hadn't passed the boards. The doctor did some sleuthing and learned from a dentist on the Board of Dental Examiners that they had flunked Dad on purpose. My mother was told, with sympathy, "Of course they flunked him. They didn't want another Jew practicing in Winston-Salem."

Though she knew it would be painful, my mother told Dad the truth of what she had learned.

Dad wept. My mother said, "It was the only time I ever saw him cry." The irony was that Dad had been a church-going Southern Baptist since before the two were married. My parents had to regroup and decide what to do next.

Danville, Virginia, on the North Carolina border, advertised for a dentist to serve in the public health department. It was as close as my parents could get to North

Carolina, so Dad took the Virginia dental boards to qualify and passed handily.

That's how we ended up in Danville, the town that would never let Dad forget his roots. I grew up there and felt that I was straddling a deep chasm—Judaism, music, intellect, and travel on one side and Southern Baptism, guilt, boredom, and attempts at conformity on the other.

## 3

Danville was a town you drove through on your way to somewhere else, the border town between North Carolina and points north. It was a textile and tobacco town with a Confederate pedigree: in April 1865, Danville's Sutherlin mansion was Jefferson Davis's headquarters for seven days after he fled Richmond just ahead of Union troops. The town still takes pride in its weeklong reign as "the Last Capital of the Confederacy."

Main Street, studded with grand ginger-breaded Victorian houses, looks much the same as it did in the latter part of the nineteenth century. First Baptist Church nestles among the historic homes. You pass the Sutherlin mansion when you drive down Main Street. In my time, it was the public library. There's a plaque in front stating, "This, The Former Home of Major W. T. Sutherlin, Is Regarded As The Last Capital Of The Confederacy, April 3-10, 1865. Here President Davis Stayed And Here Was Held The Last Full Cabinet Meeting ..."

In 1955, Danville was a one-company town. That company was Dan River Mills, the biggest employer in the region, providing more than fourteen thousand jobs for Danvillians during the decades after WWII. When you crossed the river over the Robert E. Lee Bridge connecting north and south Danville, you could tell what dye batches were being run at the mill. Just below the dam, the river flowed red or inky blue along its banks, the band of color bordered by piles of bubbles that, if you squinted your eyes, you could think of as sea foam. I thought it was a terrible thing to do to a river, and I knew that people couldn't swim in it because of the dye. Nevertheless, I saw people fishing from its banks, though it's hard to believe fish could live in such an environment, or be edible.

If you drove south on Riverside Drive and looked right, you saw, looming on a rocky outcropping in the middle of the river, the huge blue letters heralding Dan River Mills. They glowed luridly in the night sky.

Tobacco auctions marked the dwindling of summer in the "World's Best Tobacco Market." Then, the sweet smell of cured tobacco hung in the moist air, blanketing the area.

By the '60s, Riverside Drive was the place to be seen in a car, preferably a Mustang convertible, after the model came out in 1964. The town's teens hung out at the drive-up hamburger stands that lined the road. The Quick-ee-Shop was our family's favorite, where a hamburger was thirty cents. The owner was one of Dad's patients, so he gave us extra fries for free when we pulled up in the red and white '57 Chevy station wagon we affectionately dubbed "Bullet." It was a misnomer since Bullet sported a white top over a red body and looked like an upended bathtub on wheels.

Danville was full of church-going folk, about forty thousand souls who believed that Sunday was best set aside for morning and evening church services, pot-lucks, and doing nothing. The town had more churches per square mile than any other city or town in Virginia. In addition to the prevailing Baptist churches—with names like Mt. Herman, Mt. Gilead, Mt. Olive, and Gethsemane—Danville had one Catholic church and two synagogues.

Though most of Danville's churches were Baptist,

not all Baptist churches were equal. There were "high Baptist" and fundamentalist Baptist churches, the former led by divinity-school-credentialed pastors, the latter by anyone who could preach a good fire-and-brimstone sermon. My family belonged to both over the years, first to a fundamentalist church with a scare-you-to-Jesus preacher, then to a high Baptist church—West Main— with a PhD pastor.

When I was growing up, there were only 225 Jews in the Danville population. Despite their miniscule numbers, Jews were considered enough of a threat to warrant neighborhood covenants in Beverstone, Pine Tag, and Druid Hills barring blacks and Jews.

Jews couldn't belong to the Danville Country Club. The few Catholics in town didn't fare much better; they were outsiders with strange religious practices and— worst of all to a Southern Baptist—they drank alcohol. Episcopalians did, too—and they danced! My mother called them "whiskeypalians."

Danville, City of Churches and the Last Capital of the Confederacy, was also a town that brutally put down demonstrators peacefully protesting during the Civil Rights Movement when I was a young teen. Though not as well-known as Birmingham or Selma, Danville made the national news by deploying water cannons and nightsticks to injure innocent protesters kneeling to pray. Stuart Grant, the female owner of Danville's daily paper, *The Register & Bee*, was a staunch segregationist who chose not to cover what would become known as the Danville Movement.

❀❀❀❀❀

I was just about to enter first grade when we moved to Danville in the summer of 1954, bringing along the gray

*The author with her cat Fuzzy. Seeing him born taught her something about the birds and the bees. Fuzzy lived to be 21 years old.*

kitten I had named Fuzzy. Watching his birth, along with the rest of the litter, was my first introduction to the birds and the bees. From my vantage point, though, there was just one bodily outlet that produced solid-looking things, and I was puzzled about why kittens came out instead of what we in our family called "a stinky job."

We were a family of five by then, and our house was a small white frame rental on Hylton Avenue in North Danville. In his role as Danville's only public health dentist, Dad did not earn a big salary. Within a year of moving to Danville, he opened his own practice. We stayed on in North Danville, moving to three different houses in five years.

Instead of railroad tracks, Danville had the muddy Dan River to divide the town by class and race. The south side of the river was mostly white middle and upper middle class; the north side was working class, with neighborhoods built near Dan River Mills, the town's main industry. Much of the town's black population lived in the Al Magro and Pohouse Hill neighborhoods, also in North Danville.

North Danville had its own business district, a smaller, less gussied version than the one south of the river, making it look as if there were two Danvilles. In a sense, there were, because North Danville had once been a textile town called Schoolfield, which was not annexed by Danville until 1951. The whole town had been built by Riverside Cotton Mills, which was, in the early 1900s, the largest textile mill in the South.

The two Danvilles rarely met. Race and class knew their places.

For the time being, our place was on Hylton Avenue. My memory of the house consists mostly of the large attic fan set in the hall ceiling. It pulled the humid summer air through the screened window in my bedroom at night, making a slight wind over my sticky body. My mother had two-year-old Mary and my infant brother to care for, so she left me to my own devices. I roamed freely in the woods and fields near our first house. I liked to play make-believe, plucking the dried stalks of plants in the field, locating a clearing and laying out a house plan with sticks and moss to define the different rooms. In my imagination, my house was bigger than the one we lived in, and it had three bedrooms, so I had a room of my own and didn't have to share one with a two-year-old. Crouching in the field at dusk, I watched the lights of our house come on and smelled the aroma of cooking wafting out the open kitchen window and screen door. My mother called me in to supper, as she did on so many of those summer evenings when I played alone outside.

When Dad got home from work, he sometimes tiptoed into the kitchen before dinner and slid his arms around Mom from behind, when she was facing the stove.

"Oh, Hugh," Mom giggled. "Stop that."

Dad was playful that way, and I could tell from her reaction that Mom liked it.

After dinner, my mother placed a step stool in front

of the sink and directed me to wash the dinner dishes, rinse, and place them in the metal drying rack beside the sink. Having regular chores at an early age was a central tenet of my mother's child-rearing philosophy. Religious indoctrination, chores, and switchings for bad behavior were the trifecta of her parenting manifesto.

If Dad had any child-rearing philosophy, I never knew it. He went along with whatever my mother decided. Sometimes, he would threaten to take off his belt and give one of us kids a hiding, but he never followed through. He was the fun guy who played checkers with me, tossed me a ball, and carried me on his shoulders out beyond the breakers when we started going to Nags Head on the North Carolina Outer Banks in the summers.

❖❖❖❖❖

When I started first grade at G.L.H. Johnson Elementary School, I developed a phobia about my first name, Mirinda. It set me apart from the Sues, the Sandras, the Janets, and the Junes. I speculated that my parents preferred Jean, because it was one syllable and easier to summon me with. It was bad enough to have a foreign sounding last name like Kossoff, so I clung to Jean, a blend-in name.

When the teacher called the roll each morning, she used students' full names. I waited queasily as she went through the A's to the K's. Then came Mirinda Jean Kossoff, and I shrank in my seat, squeaking out a "here." Though teachers and students called me Jean, I didn't like it that they knew my first name.

My first year in grammar school, 1954, was also the year Hurricane Hazel wreaked havoc with a direct hit on North Carolina, including border towns like Danville. Dad came to my school to rescue me.

"Jean, your Dad's here," my teacher said, as other children were filing from the classroom to meet their parents. I knew it had been raining hard, but I had no idea what my school parking lot looked like. I was just happy that Dad had come for me.

Dad grabbed my hand. "Hurry up," he said. "We have to get out of here."

He led me to the door, then scooped me up and carried me to the car, as he waded through ankle-deep and rising water. I felt warm and safe in those arms, certain that he would always be there to rescue me when I needed him. I needed him often.

⚡⚡⚡⚡

As a first- and second-grader, I came down with a series of childhood illnesses—chicken pox, scarlet fever, even a mild case of polio that fortunately did no permanent damage. My mother took great care of me when I was sick. That was the only time I got her undivided attention, but she didn't have the breezy, reassuring tone that Dad used when treating cuts and skinned knees, like the time I was running to catch up with the Good Humor truck, so I could fork over a nickel for my favorite cherry popsicle. I stumbled at the curb and went down on both hands, splitting open my right palm on a rock. I ran home crying. As soon as the screen door banged behind me, and Mom saw me dripping blood, she yelled, "Hugh, come look at Jean's hand."

"Well, here's the walking wounded." Dad examined my palm with an air of professional detachment. "We'll wash it out, put some Merthiolate on it, and you'll be back chasing the Good Humor man tomorrow." Dad laughed, but Merthiolate was no laughing matter. That was the part of the treatment I fervently wished to avoid.

"It's gonna sting," I wailed.

"Don't kvetch. This'll only take a minute." He used the same cool efficiency, sometimes sparked with a witticism, in treating our wounds as he did in the office while filling or extracting teeth, doing root canals, or fitting a patient for dentures.

When my siblings were too young for it, I played checkers with Dad. We kept a tally of who won and lost. I won often. Maybe he let me win. At the time, I was certain I won fair and square because I could think several moves ahead and always had him on the defensive. At least I thought so. This gave me great pleasure.

We faced each other across my low play table. "I know where you're going with that and it won't work," Dad teased.

"Just watch me," I said. "I've got you cornered now."

"Hey, I didn't see that!" he exclaimed.

I smiled, basking in his attention.

My time with Dad was special. I was the oldest and the one who looked most like him. We were cut from the same cloth, he and I.

❧❧❧❧❧

By the time I reached third grade, we moved to a larger brick bungalow on Norwood Drive, also in North Danville, and I went to Schoolfield Grammar School.

Two daughters and Dad's long-hoped-for son required a house with at least three bedrooms. My youngest sister, Jane, ten years my junior, had yet to be born. Once again, I had to share a room with Mary so our brother could have his own room. Mary was messy and I was neat, so I drew a chalk line on the wood floor between my side of the room and hers and dared her to cross it with her junk. Every piece of her flotsam and jetsam had to stay behind the line on her side of the bedroom.

When Mary and I couldn't sleep, I launched the number game: I would think of a number between one and twenty and tell my sister to concentrate and come up with the number I was thinking of. She went along with this beginning ESP experiment. Sometimes Mary made a hit; most often she didn't, but we were always eager to improve the odds. I thought maybe she could tune into me and get the right number every time—or I could get on her wavelength, because we took turns.

Our other bedtime game was for one of us to rap out the rhythm to a song on our matching white Naugahyde headboards and get the other to guess the tune. Sometimes it would be Mitch Miller's "The Yellow Rose of Texas" or Sheb Wooley's "The Purple People Eater." And of course Elvis's "Don't be Cruel." This was less successful than the ESP experiment, because rhythms were tricky, and they were the only clue.

My favorite books had become Lewis Carroll's *Alice's Adventure in Wonderland* and *Through the Looking-Glass.*

The concept of another world—and a big adventure—on the other side of the looking glass fascinated me, so much so that I spent some time in front of mirrors trying to pass through. I was a girl in search of adventure, but it would have to come later in life.

## 4

As I grew older, instead of lullabies, Dad serenaded me with World War II songs like "Over There," or a version of "She Wore a Yellow Ribbon."

*Around her neck, she wore a yellow ribbon; she wore it in December and in the month of May, and if you asked her why the heck she wore it; she wore it for that airman who was far, far away; far away, far away; Oh, she wore it for that airman who was far, far away.*

That was my favorite of Dad's repertoire of songs. I knew he had been that airman far away and had lived to tell of his narrow escapes during the war. An air of death-defying adventure still clung to him, and I could almost feel it. I wanted adventure, too, but something less scary than Dad's.

Eventually, bedtime storybooks gave way to real tales of World War II adventures starring my father. The cast included Dad's best friend, Bev Morris, the ball turret gunner, and Ken Bridenstein, the pilot. Dad was the top turret gunner and flight engineer. The setting was the cockpit of a B-17 bomber. The crew was stationed in England, members of the Army Air Corps, Eighth Air Force, 286th bomb group. Their mission was to bomb targets in Germany.

"We were flying in formation, two other American bombers spaced at intervals below," Dad said. "I saw the lowest B-17 take a direct hit and break apart in a fiery explosion. The exploding fragments knocked out the plane flying just below us. It was the saddest day of my life when I got back to the barracks that night and saw all those empty bunks."

That anecdote always got to me, but in the telling of it, Dad showed little emotion. I thought about those empty bunks, the beds of airmen who didn't come back alive, and I was sad.

As bomber pilots, Dad and his crewmates were shielded by distance from the deaths they wrought. They could see smoke rising when they hit targets below, but the destruction was faceless and impersonal.

But at least once, death had a face, and it was that of a young German pilot. "During one mission," Dad told me, "we were in a dogfight with a formation of Messerschmitts. One came up beside us, so close I could see the pilot. I fired twice, but the bullets bounced off the metal below his cockpit. Then I raised the level of the gun and saw the bullets smash through the cockpit and hit the pilot. I could see his blond hair sticking out from under his head-gear." Dad's voice lowered. "Then I saw him slump over the steering wheel, and his plane went into a nosedive."

"Dad, were you sorry you killed him?"

"It was him or us," Dad replied, matter-of-factly. "And I was going to make sure it wasn't us."

In my mind, I saw that blond German pilot and imagined the blood spilling from his head. I never heard the story without feeling it viscerally, as though I'd been there.

The best and most oft-repeated account was about the time Dad almost didn't make it back to base.

"We were over Berlin," he said. His eyes got that distant look, as if he were watching a movie reel inside his head. I didn't like it when he went deep into those memories. Even though he was there with me physically, his attention was somewhere else.

"Tracers streaked the sky, and there was anti-aircraft fire from below. We took so many hits I lost count. The plane was riddled with bullet holes, and each time we got hit, we thought that would be the one that brought us down." Dad frowned, his eyebrows knit together. I held my breath in anticipation of the rest of the story.

"For the first time in my life," Dad said, "I prayed hard, and I told God that if he saved us and got us back to base, I would become a Christian. He did, and I lived up to my part of the bargain."

"So you became a Christian then, Dad? Before you married Mom?"

"That's right."

"Jesus saved you, then?"

"Yes, he did."

I never thought to ask Dad if it had been hard for him to give up being a Jew in order to become a Christian. I had only known him as a Baptist. And he was a Baptist because my mother was a Baptist. Since he went to church with my mother before shipping out, Dad was familiar with Baptist rituals when he made his promise to God. As an adult, I wondered, after he saw what happened to millions of his tribe during the war, if he felt relieved to flee to the perceived safety of Christianity.

I could picture him in the turret of his B-17, slicing the sky as tracers lit up the night like fireworks, bullets cracking through the plane's fuselage, my father's terror. What would it have been like to be in the turret of a B-17, taking enemy fire—heart pounding, ears ringing, muscles knotted, and crewmates depending on you to get back alive? My dad was a hero.

Other war stories I heard later from my brother, because they were too off-color for Dad to tell me himself— like the time he had an attack of diarrhea while on a mission. He emptied his cramping bowels in a cardboard box on the plane. The rest of the crew groaned about the smell and directed Dad to dump the box out of the bay doors. When he did, the contents got caught in the plane's slipstream and splattered over the bubble of the ball turret.

My father's tales served to pique my romantic vision of the '40s—a vision I was already creating from the movies and music of the time. I wished I had lived then—when men and women fell in love urgently in the face of an uncertain future; when war buddies stared down death together, forging unbreakable bonds; when the country was united and men like my father were welcomed home as heroes. I loved war movies like *The Bridge on the River Kwai* with William Holden and Alec Guinness and *The Longest Day* and *The Sands of Iwo Jima* with John Wayne.

I swooned over love songs like Vera Lynn's rendition of "I'll Be Seeing You." The song was about heartache and longing arising from being separated from the one you love, the one you may never see again. Even then, I knew that separation and uncertainty intensified such feelings.

My love of the era and my romantic fantasies about it developed and were embellished over time, until I hit adolescence. Then I considered those war stories nothing but old stories I'd heard many times before. I was more concerned with boys and fitting in. Besides, Dad had shifted his attention to my brother Roger, and I felt sidelined.

## 5

Grandpa Herman's stories always fascinated me. He was born on April 2, 1892, in Belarus and came to the United States in 1897.

In Russia, his first name was Hyman and surname Kossowoi or Kosovoy, which must have been changed when the family landed, via Liverpool, on the shores of America. Family lore was that his father, Isaac, had been in the Russian army and wounded himself with his own saber in order to escape the yoke of servitude and mistreatment Jews suffered under the last imperial rulers. Isaac brought his young son—my grandfather— with him and settled in Manhattan's Lower East Side on Delancey Street, where Isaac worked as a tailor. Isaac's wife Yetta arrived two years later, along with their daughter Mary and son Jacob. Their younger two daughters, my great-aunts Ida and Dora, were born in the United States.

Grandpa Herman sported a small dark mustache and a thick crest of dark hair. A slight gap in his front teeth softened the impact of the mustache. His dress was more European than American. He often wore a cravat.

Grandpa Herman was a concert pianist who studied with composer Leopold Godowsky in Vienna. He spoke four languages fluently—English, French, German, and Italian—as well as a smattering of his native Russian. When he traveled to Europe every summer, he always sailed from New York harbor to Calais on one of his

*Grandpa Herman was a concert pianist who studied with
composer Leopold Godowsky in Vienna as a young man.*

favorite Dutch passenger liners. These trips were usually solo. He left Dad, as a child, and Grandma Sadye,
behind.

Grandpa Herman and Grandma Sadye visited us every spring. Mom never seemed pleased about their visits
and was usually grouchy in anticipation of their arrival.
She depicted Grandpa Herman as a shady character and
adulterer. She could just as easily have referred to him
as a bon vivant and intellectual, but she did not have the
imagination to see him that way. When she started in on
him, I fumed silently. I loved my worldly and intellectual
grandfather. Perhaps because I was the firstborn, we had
a special bond he didn't have with my siblings. Plus, I
was his best audience for the stories that were his coin
of the realm.

I never told my mother that I hated it when she talked
down someone I loved. I knew she would feel I was taking his side over hers.

If I could read her mind, she could read mine. She
never missed an opportunity to un-shelter me from

Grandpa's romantic life, safe from any contradiction from me. "He has mistresses all over Europe and goes by his middle name, David, when he's there. That's why he leaves your grandmother at home every summer. And that's why she suffers from those terrible depressions."

While I felt sad for Grandma Sadye and thought she should have gone to Europe, too, I'm not sure she wished to go. I didn't want to hear bad things about Grandpa Herman, or that he was responsible for her mental illness. Maybe he had mistresses in Europe, as my mother said, but that was his business. I didn't think my mother should have been telling me things to belittle him in my eyes. Even as a child, I knew it was wrong of her, and I knew that I was trapped into silence.

⚜⚜⚜⚜⚜

I was told that Grandma Sadye sometimes went into catatonic states in which she wouldn't or couldn't speak and that these depressive episodes often coincided with Grandpa's approaching summer trips to Europe. I never saw her in such a state, but paid attention to what my parents said about her. Shock therapy was the only treatment that would bring her back. I didn't question Grandpa's decision to go alone, but, as my mother had drilled into me, I suspected his preparations to leave triggered Grandma's depression. In front of me, Dad never agreed or disagreed with this theory. He remained neutral, almost detached, caught between my mother's judgment and loyalty to his father. I sympathized with him and felt that he and I were allies.

Grandma Sadye's mental illness was not discussed or labeled as such. I thought of her bouts of severe depression as just one of Grandma's traits. I didn't understand that she was one of many who suffered from mental illness or that depression such as hers was a serious and life-altering illness.

I don't know how many times she endured shock therapy treatments. My parents mentioned Grandma Sadye's treatments matter-of-factly, as if she'd gone into the hospital for an appendectomy, was discharged and then, after a short recovery, was fine. It was an era when mental illness was a stain upon a family, so I don't wonder that my parents brushed it off in front of us children. But I knew Dad was concerned about her and phoned Grandpa regularly about her progress.

Grandpa Herman brought me gifts from Europe—a red beanie with edelweiss stitched onto it, a Swiss music box, and when I was a teenager, French perfume— Réplique by Raphael Paris. With him, I felt special in a way I didn't feel with my parents. He lavished attention on me, the kind of attention I was hungry for. He treated me as a kid with smarts who didn't need talking down to. On his knee, I learned my first French phrase: *Mademoiselle, vous etes très gentil.*

"What does that mean, Grandpa?"

"It means, Miss, you are very kind."

I would use that phrase often, and not just in the proper context, throughout my life.

I loved and admired him for his accomplishments and the fact that he saw something special in me. I think he had high hopes for me, even though I was being reared in a Gentile home in a small Southern town without much culture. He told me about Vienna before the war, about Italian art and German music. As he talked—and he talked a lot—small quarter moons of spittle gathered at the corners of his mouth. I thought of them as Grandpa's talking corners, like little bits of masonry to keep his lips from flying apart. No one else I knew had them.

*Grandpa Herman in mid-life, as the author knew him. He was intelligent, worldly, well traveled, and voluble. When visiting, he always brought gifts and his "medicine cabinet," a portable leather liquor cabinet, for his nightcap.*

Grandpa Herman and Grandma Sadye made the annual drive from New York to Danville in their black Buick sedan with a chrome grill that looked like a cartoonish grin. When Grandpa pulled in behind our Chevy station wagon in the driveway, I sidled up to the driver's side door as he got out, the smell of gasoline exhaust lingering in the air.

"*Ah, ma petite choux-choux,*" he said. "It's your foxy old grandpa." And then he kissed me, his clothes smelling of old leather suitcases, his mustache prickling my cheek. He walked around the car to open the door for Grandma Sadye.

I ran over to hug tiny Grandma Sadye. She smelled like Ivory soap and something else indefinable—a scent that was neither pleasant nor unpleasant. It was simply *eau de* Grandma Sadye.

She seemed frail, supported on bird legs sheathed in transparent skin mapped with prominent blue veins that I could see through her stockings. At the end of her left arm was a dollop of flesh with tiny nubs for fingers, a congenital birth defect. She kept her left hand glued to her waist, draped in a hanky to hide it from prying eyes. I was curious about that little hand, and I thought of it the way I considered my doll's hand—tiny, pink, and cute. I wasn't repelled by it; on the contrary, I wanted to touch and play with the little finger stubs, but I understood that she would have been embarrassed by that kind of attention. Sometimes her little hand emerged to wash dishes or twist her long gray hair into a bun at the base of her neck, and I marveled at how dexterous she was with it. And her teeth—how like piano keys they were— large and squared off, the color of the ivories on the old upright piano we had acquired after one of our moves to larger quarters.

❧❧❧❧❧

"You want to drive the Buick?" Grandpa asked when I was six or seven. I beamed.

"Oh yes, can I, please?"

He tucked me into the passenger side of the car and slid in behind the wheel. I scooted next to him, and he lifted me under the steering column to sit on his lap. I could just see over the wheel. After that maneuver, we proceeded to drive slowly around the block, my hands, along with his, on the wheel. My smile felt as big as the Buick's chrome grill.

His hands were beautiful—muscular but sensitive, with lean tapering fingers, perfect hands for a pianist. As a young man, he took to the concert stage but eventually settled into being an exacting and revered piano teacher in New York.

I knew about the exacting part, because he terrorized me into making more progress at the piano in a week with him than I did during months with my Danville teacher. He sat beside me on the bench of our old upright piano and paid attention to every detail of my playing: "Repeat those two measures; make the notes flow into each other. You're playing a line that rises and falls."

If I didn't do it exactly right on the second try, I feared he'd rap my knuckles. He instilled in me a passion for Chopin, Beethoven, and Brahms.

With the requisite amount of begging, he would play for us. My favorite piece, among the non-classics, was his rendition of "Autumn Leaves," because it's about Paris and lovers. When he played it, I could see in his eyes that he went there—Paris, the city I dreamt of seeing, too. In Paris, there would be lovers walking along the Seine, the smell of French perfume, sophisticated women in the latest fashions strolling the avenues, artists and musicians, and worldliness. I pledged to myself then that I would go to Paris someday.

But usually, he'd play Chopin or one of his favorites, Beethoven's "Moonlight Sonata," humming as he played.

For breakfast, he liked kippers and brown bread. Both were exotic for Danville and my mother scoured the area supermarkets and stores to find them. While she did her best to cater to my grandparents' tastes, she anticipated their disapproval and resented it.

"When your grandparents go to their bedroom, behind closed doors, they criticize us," Mom said. "The house isn't this, or the food isn't that. They've never approved of me." I heard this with every visit.

Mom's claims gave me an idea. "Let's get some glasses from the kitchen," I told Roger and Mary, "and listen against the wall to their bedroom after they go to bed."

That same night, drinking glasses in hand, we tiptoed to the adjacent bedroom—my brother's—and gently put our drinking glasses against the wall separating the two rooms.

I put a finger to my lips as we tried to keep from laughing. Despite listening intently, we only heard snatches of conversation and were unable to confirm or deny my mother's suspicions. We tiptoed out of the room, none the wiser.

Once exposed to it, my grandparents became fond of Southern food. Their favorite restaurant in town was Mary's Diner, or "Aunt Mary's" as they called it, a diner with a serving line that dished out fried chicken, grits, green beans, and Dad's favorite—banana pudding.

After dinner, and close to our bedtime, Grandpa Herman followed his nightly ritual. Because liquor was forbidden in our Baptist household, Grandpa would rub his hands together and say, "It's time for my medicine."

He toted his portable leather liquor cabinet into our knotty-pine den, placed it on the table and opened it like a large upright book on hinges. I was fascinated by the small cups and the miniature silver flasks lined up inside. Like a magician, he mixed elixirs into a cup and came up with a potion that pleased him. He took a seat with a smile and smacked his lips over the first sip, saying, "Ah, this is good for the old ticker."

My mother often said to me, "You look just like Grandpa Herman when you do that." Or, "That expression is just like Grandpa Herman." Once in a while, she even called me "little Herman." The way she said it let me know that it wasn't a good thing to be compared to Grandpa Herman. I came to understand that showing too much love or loyalty to Grandpa Herman was a betrayal of my mother, who never knew her real father and who would never enjoy the same approval that I received from Grandpa.

As I was the oldest and the only one of the four children she compared to Grandpa Herman, I began to feel set apart from my brother and sisters—and not in a good way. My brother and sisters didn't have much interest in what Grandpa Herman had to offer. They gratefully accepted his latest gifts from Italy, France, or Switzerland but then moved on. Perhaps he'd always treated me differently because I looked more like the Jewish side of my family—with my dark hair, distinctive eyebrows that, like Dad's, grew to a point in the middle, and a smaller, shorter version of his nose. Above all, I had an insatiable curiosity and a passion to travel, piqued by his stories.

The family ties were not broken, just frayed, when my grandparents visited.

When I was twelve, Grandpa said he would take me with him to Europe the following summer. I was thrilled at the prospect of finally seeing Paris and being with someone who spoke that beautiful language.

My imagination was on steroids. After he returned to New York, I wrote him a letter full of girlish anticipation. His answer was to write something about me and "my dollar dreams" and to never mention taking me to Europe again. I was embarrassed and thought that I had made a mistake in assuming he would take me with him. Though I was hurt, I blamed myself. My mother's response hurt more: "He was never going to take you to Europe; you'd just be in his way."

This took some of the shine off Grandpa Herman. I began to understand that he wasn't perfect, either.

≈≈≈≈≈ 6 ≈≈≈≈≈

Throughout my childhood, until I was sixteen, Grandma C, as we called Mom's mother, spent a couple of months each year with us. The rest of the year, she lived with my mother's twin, Martha, helping her care for her two sons—my cousins David and Joe. When I think of Grandma C, I picture her in one of our lounge chairs, head tilted back, eyes closed, snoring with her mouth open. Once, I shared a bed with her at Aunt Martha's house and was impressed to discover that she still used a chamber pot, which she kept under the bed, even though a half bath was just inside her bedroom.

Grandma C had married a widower with six children. My grandfather, Ira Whitfield, died in the great influenza epidemic of 1918, leaving Grandma with the six stepchildren and the twins they had together—my mother and aunt. After Ira's death, my grandmother moved with the children to the National Orphans Home in Tiffin, Ohio. She got a job at the orphanage and was there four years until she succumbed to the wooing of a certain widowed farmer named Rufus Covington, who regularly wrote to her from North Carolina.

After she agreed to return to North Carolina and marry him, Rufus suggested she leave her twins at the orphanage. Grandma C was adamant that they come with her or no deal. She prevailed. The marriage seemed to be one of convenience: Grandma needed the financial support of a husband and Rufus needed someone

*Elsie Whitfield, later Grandma C, with her twins, Nancy Ozelle, the author's mother, on the left, and Martha Mozelle on the right. This photo was likely taken the same year that Ira Whitfield, Elsie's husband and the author's grandfather, died in the influenza epidemic of 1918.*

to help him work the farm. Eventually, he, too, passed on, widowing my grandmother a second time. By then, my mother and her twin were old enough to make their own way.

Grandma C never had been a beauty. In old photos, her face is severe, with droopy eyes that looked like they were circled with soot. Her mouth drooped, too. She wore her dark hair pinned to the top of her head. Old age softened her features, but by then she was as round as she was tall, and her nose had broadened. The severity of her fundamentalist beliefs remained unchanged.

The cushion of Grandma C's waist was a stark contrast to Grandma Sadye's bony little frame. Neither was a warm and demonstrative grandmother. Hugging was generally confined to an initial greeting, though I was around Grandma C more often and made a point of bestowing hugs and kisses in hopes of getting some in return. It was a one-way street. The one concession she made was to allow me to brush out her long, wavy gray-white hair at night. Every morning, she put it up in a bun again.

Like Grandma Sadye, Grandma C was an excellent cook, but in the Southern tradition. I helped her make apple pies. Grandma C peeled winesaps, her knife working around the apple until the skin came off in one big spiral. She rolled her own crust and sifted together cinnamon and sugar to coat each apple slice, topped by generous dots of butter. When the filling was complete, she gently laid down the top crust, crimping the edges with fork tines and piercing the top to let out steam and bubbling bits of caramelized apple juice. Once a year, near Thanksgiving when the fruit was ripe, Grandma C made persimmon pudding. You had to pick the persimmons at just the right time. Too early and they would be so bitter as to be inedible.

Grandma C's father, Efram Holler, was a circuit-riding Baptist minister who pastored four churches in Wilkes County, North Carolina, visiting each one on horseback once a month. When his far-flung congregations didn't have cash, they paid Efram with baked goods, beans, yams, chickens, eggs, or a slab of pork. Grassy Knob Baptist Church near North Wilkesboro was the church closest to the Holler home. Grandma C told me that often, after Efram had delivered his sermon, he would leap on a stump in the churchyard and invite any who were within earshot to Sunday dinner at his house nearby.

Great-grandmother Nancy Mirinda Holler (Granny Holler) made enormous platters of chicken and fresh vegetables from their garden, not only for the visitors, but also to feed her ten children. They were not well off, but they did have plenty of food. Great-granddad believed in sharing what the Lord provided.

Grandma C liked to talk about the characters who came to feast at Granny Holler's bountiful table. One oft-repeated tale involved a local ne'er-do-well and his son. They were chowing down to a meal of fried chicken, beans, and potatoes when the boy piped up and said, "Dad steals his potatoes."

"Yes," the father replied. "Dad peels his potatoes."

Grandma C's ample belly shook with laughter after she delivered the punch line. It was infectious. I laughed, too. I felt the closest to Grandma C when she was regaling us with stories from her life.

When it came to men, Grandma C's favorite description was, "You know, that man was as ugly as a mud fence daubed with lizards."

Another story involved a parishioner asking Granny Holler how she could have so many children when her husband was away much of the time preaching.

"Well, I was just so glad to see him when he did get home," she replied, laughing.

Grandma C had the gift of healing, or laying-on of hands. She had been known as the medicine woman in her Pilot Mountain, North Carolina, community, ministering to the sick with her homemade remedies and washing and preparing the dead for burial. Mom swore that, as a child, she had seen Grandma C make tumors disappear from those who sought her help. This she did with a secret ceremony involving prayer and scripture, and one of her salves. Mom only witnessed the results, not the ceremony.

Granddaddy Holler had been a healer, and he handed down the knowledge and the sacrament to Grandma C. He chose her for this honor from among the ten siblings. The sacrament, my mother said, was passed down from father to daughter and from mother to son, alternating gender with each generation. Since she had only stepsons, Grandma C tried to "pass the blessing" to Dad, but said she could not because he wasn't a blood relative. The fact that she wanted to spoke volumes about how much she esteemed Dad. He was fond of her, too,

*Young
Nancy
Ozelle
Whitfield
on the
farm.*

and always treated her with respect. He was happy to have her live with us part-time.

He never mentioned the meeting with Grandma C or the failure of her attempts to pass on her healing ceremony. I remember seeing the two of them go behind closed doors and wondering why. Afterward, my mother told me what had happened, but not in detail.

Whatever the blessing was, it died with her. As the oldest daughter, who would be next in line to learn the secret, I felt cheated of my birthright, especially since Dad would not answer my questions about the ceremony or what happened between him and Grandma C. He was good at clamming up. I learned from experience that pushing made no difference. What would happen if I pushed too hard? I didn't want to know.

By the time I was old enough to go to school, both my mother and aunt had grown into plump women who wore their brown hair cut at ear length. I thought my mother the better looking of the two. She looked more like her father, Ira Whitfield, from the few pictures I'd seen of him. Aunt Martha looked more like Grandma C.

Mom was jealous because Grandma C spent more time with Aunt Martha's family than with ours. Aunt Martha worked outside the home, as a nurse on the night shift, so I assumed Grandma felt more needed at her house. Mom took it as rejection, as she tended to take anything that didn't go her way, saying Grandma C loved Martha more than her.

Aunt Martha, in turn, was jealous of Mom and her cushy life. My cousin Joe told me he often heard his mother say, "We're not like them. We don't bow down to the almighty dollar." When, after Uncle Walter died, Mom paid for a trip to Europe for herself and Aunt Martha, my aunt said Mom was "too controlling." I thought Mom had been generous.

When I was sixteen, a tearful Aunt Martha called Mom to tell her to get to the hospital in Winston-Salem quickly. Grandma C had a blood clot in her aorta. She made it through surgery, but a few days later, her exhausted old body gave out. I rode with my mother to the hospital, more than an hour's drive away. When we arrived, my mother and aunt fell upon each other and wept. Grandma C had died before we got there.

We went into the hospital room to see Grandma C one last time before the hearse took her away. I was reluctant to see my dead grandmother, but I knew Mom and Aunt Martha expected me to pay my respects. Grandma C lay on the hospital bed with her white hair arrayed around her like a halo. My mother told me to kiss her. I didn't want to kiss a dead body. This wasn't Grandma C anymore, but I knuckled under to please my mother and leaned down to put my lips on Grandma's cheek. Her skin was not warm and soft as in life, but chill and unyielding. Immediately, I backed away. After my mother and aunt kissed and stroked Grandma's head, we left.

I had seen one other dead person, a schoolmate who drowned at seven years old. I, along with other friends, was asked to carry flowers to set by her open casket at the service. I saw her swollen face against the satin pillow. I had nightmares for weeks afterward. Grandma C's passing was not frightening in that way. Instead, it left a hole in our lives. She had been the link connecting us to our past. She had been part of our daily lives for years, and I would miss her hearty laugh, her stories, and her apple pies.

## 7

Religion was entwined in our family life. Dad embraced the fundamentalist Baptist faith with fervor. We attended North Main Baptist Church on Sunday mornings, Sunday evenings, and Wednesday evening prayer services. I found these services boring and repetitive. I doodled on the church programs, waiting eagerly for Preacher Jones to finish his sermon and "amen" us into the final hymn. "Blest Be the Tie That Binds" was a frequent one, and I liked to belt it out with the grown-ups. The music appealed to me and kept me from going bonkers at the services. That was until a revival preacher came to North Main when I was eleven years old and got my attention.

Preacher Gibbs was a tall red-haired man with a ruddy complexion and a booming voice—a voice bigger than his stature. He was already perspiring inside his dark suit when he took the podium. The full church was warm and smelled of sweat and perfume. The women stirred the air with their church fans. On one side, the cardboard fans had a picture of Jesus in a white robe, with long flowing brown hair, knocking on a cottage door. The reverse side said "Jesus Saves" and "North Main Baptist Church."

"You were born in sin, but God the loving father sent his son Jesus to save you from your sins," Preacher Gibbs thundered, pointing a condemning finger at me and the rest of the congregation. "The fires of hell await those who do not repent and accept Jesus into their hearts.

"After Judas betrays Jesus with a kiss, the Romans arrest him, and Pontius Pilate sentences him to death. The Romans lash Jesus with leather whips and put a crown of thorns on his head and mockingly call him 'the King of the Jews.' He staggers under the weight of carrying the cross. Jesus is drenched with blood and sweat, so weak that Simon of Cyrene helps him shoulder the burden of the cross. When Jesus reaches Golgotha, the Romans strip him of his robe. They lay him on the cross and nail his feet and hands to the wood. Blood flows from Jesus's wounds as they raise the cross. But Jesus forgives his tormentors. He says 'Father, forgive them for they know not what they do.'"

I held my breath, my eyes laser focused on Preacher Gibbs and beginning to well up.

"Jesus comforts a thief on the cross beside him and tells him, 'Today, thou wilt be with me in paradise.' Jesus suffers in agony, bleeding and struggling for breath, his head hung low over his chest. Mary, his mother, is sobbing at the foot of the cross. At the ninth hour, he cries out, 'My God, my God, why hast thou forsaken me?' In taking on the sins of the world, Jesus is for the first time separated from God the Father; it is a terrible thing," Preacher Gibbs intoned. "Jesus says, 'I thirst,' but he is only given a sop of vinegar. Then a Roman soldier drives a sword into his side, and water flows. A short time later, Jesus says, 'It is finished. Father into thy hands I commend my spirit.'"

By that time, imagining the crucifixion scene in my mind, I wondered what I had done that was so bad Jesus had to die such a horrible death for it. I didn't want Jesus to have died in vain. I wept.

Preacher Gibbs interrupted my grief. "But we know that on the third day Jesus rose from the dead. He is risen! He is at the right hand of God. Now is the time to

repent of your sins and accept Jesus as your savior. Won't
you come, come to the altar and accept the love and for-
giveness of Christ who died for you so that you might live
life eternal? Won't you come to Jesus now?"

The organ played "Just as I Am." *Just as I am without
one plea, but that thy blood was shed for me—*. The music
pushed me over the edge.

With my heart pounding so hard that my hands shook,
I stood up, first bent at the waist, and then straighten-
ing a little. I left my parents' side and stayed partially
bent over to avoid too much attention. I crawled across
a few people to the end of the pew. They made room
for me. They and my parents knew what I was doing,
but I couldn't look at them. I was too embarrassed about
showing my tears. In our family, one didn't cry in public.

As I approached Preacher Gibbs behind a few others
who had come forward, there was a sour taste of fear in
my mouth. Thankfully, I did not have to walk the full
aisle from the back. I swallowed hard, and in a quaking
voice, I mumbled, "I want to be saved, and I accept Jesus
Christ as my savior."

Preacher Gibbs put a hand to my back, and I, along
with five or so men and women, turned to the congregation. I was the only kid among the bunch. "Blessed are
they that hunger and thirst for righteousness, for they
shall be satisfied," he said in a sing-song voice. "We welcome you brothers and sisters in Christ. You will never
die. At judgment day, your body will join your soul to live
with God eternally."

Still teary-eyed, I looked out at rows of approving faces, including those of my parents in the family row, about
halfway from the front. My brother and sister were still
in Sunday school, my toddler sister Jane in the nursery. I
figured I'd done the right thing. It was embarrassing being in front of the congregation with my cheeks still wet

with tears. But I liked being one of them and one with my parents. Grandma C would be happy.

Yet somehow, I was uneasy.

On the ride home after church, Mom said, "I'm glad you made your profession of faith today. I've been waiting for you to do that, but I didn't want to push you."

"You made the right move," Dad added, as if we had been playing checkers. I didn't know how to respond. I was glad that they were pleased, but I didn't understand what had happened or why I would be going to heaven now, when earlier, before I accepted Jesus, hell would have been my destination. I couldn't figure out the logic of it, but I knew that logic was not the point. The point was faith.

My salvation day was otherwise unremarkable. There was no celebration of my brave stand for Jesus. If I thought my world would change after I accepted Jesus, I would be disappointed. After we got home, Mom and Dad returned to their usual routine of reading the Sunday paper in bed, while I tried to figure out what to do with myself.

What I hadn't thought through during my impulsive walk to the front of the church was the terrifying prospect of baptism, soon to follow. Baptists don't tolerate a mere flick of holy water on the forehead. Oh no, Baptists have to be dunked, completely in over their heads, in a baptismal pool, behind the church altar and in front of the pews for everyone to witness. I was worried and anxious about the baptism to come, the next Sunday.

When baptism day arrived, I was in a sweat of dread. After I got to North Main with my family, a churchwoman met me and escorted me to a small anteroom with dark stained-glass windows. She handed me a white robe and told me to change into it. There were other people in the room—five grown women—but no one my age.

As we began to undress, I was shocked to see them in their underwear—slips, stockings, and garter belts, then bras and panties. I tried not to stare. I had never seen my mother in her underwear, let alone strange women. My mother always closed and locked her bedroom door when she changed clothes or got dressed in the morning.

These women had breasts—of different shapes and sizes—and I was agog. There were dimpled, chubby thighs and loose skin dangling from underarms. As I changed from my Sunday dress to the gown, I was naked on top while the others had their bras. This was distressing. I noticed my two little pink nipples on the flat plane of my chest, like a couple of raisins.

The robes we donned were made of a thin fabric. After we were all gowned up, the preacher came in to greet and pray with us. My body was tense, and I could feel the blood rise to my face.

We lined up at the entrance steps to the baptismal pool. A couple of women got dunked before me, and I noticed that their robes, when wet, were almost see-through as they climbed the steps to exit the pool. Upon making this discovery, I fantasized about bolting, but I couldn't do that to my parents.

When my turn came, I began to regret that profession of faith I had made on the previous Sunday. Beneath my white robe, I felt exposed as I descended the steps into the chest high pool, my hands busy pressing the gown down around my knees as the water threatened to make a balloon of it. The congregation would be able to see everything when I climbed the steps out of the pool.

Preacher Gibbs reached out to grab my trembling hand and pulled me toward him, the water reaching only to his upper thighs. He cupped one hand under my head and used the other to close off my nose as he slid me under the water, saying, as he had to the others, "I baptize you in the name of the Father, and of the Son, and of the Holy Spirit." I came up sputtering. "Welcome, sister, into the fold of the lambs of Jesus," he added, as I climbed the steps out of the pool. Shivering with cold, I crossed my arms around my chest. Someone, I don't remember who, waited with a towel, then led me back to the changing room and a dry pair of underpants my mother had put in a bag. Thoughts of Jesus's wounds fled my mind, leaving only the feeling of being exposed.

Finally, I got back to them after the service. "We're proud of you," Mom said, as she put an arm around my shoulders.

"Good thing you didn't drown in there," Dad quipped.

My ordeal over, I basked in their approval.

I had survived the initiation, so I could enjoy the church potluck after the service. Dad loved these potlucks and would return to the heavily laden tables again and again—fried chicken, green beans, Jello salad, macaroni and cheese, and banana pudding. I mimicked him by filling up my plate a couple of times. There was communion in sharing food, not unlike the communion I could, as a newly saved member of the tribe, partake of when celebrated at church on certain occasions.

Since we were Baptists, we drank grape juice for the blood of Christ and ate small squares of white bread to represent the body of Christ. Before my salvation, when the burnished brass trays were passed over me, I felt left out. The smell of the juice and bread made my mouth water, and I was dazzled by the highly polished brass that reflected the huge ceiling lights as the tray went by, the cups of juice arranged in circles around the center glass container that held the bread. As ritual, I couldn't grasp it. To take it seemed cannibalistic. Salvation didn't change my concept of taking communion, but I enjoyed the tiny bread squares and the little cups of grape juice, and I liked being grown-up enough to participate. When Dad was one of the deacons, he helped pass the trays. I was proud of him and intently watched him as he stood at the end of the aisles passing the body and blood of Jesus.

I had been taught that I would have eternal life in heaven when I accepted Christ as my savior, but I couldn't wrap my mind around eternal life. Many nights, I lay in bed thinking about time that never ends and living forever in heaven. I concluded that it could get quite boring. It never entered my mind to talk to my parents about it, just as I would not have told them about how I obsessed over listening to my own heartbeat. It seemed steady and purposeful, but how could I rely on it to keep up the work?

There were missionaries in our church who gave up their comfortable lives to go to far-off places like Africa and South America to convert the unbelievers. At one service, a missionary couple talked to the congregation about their experiences and the travails of living in poor countries. This was in winter, and the missionary man said he didn't have an overcoat. At the end of the service, Dad approached the man, took off his overcoat, and gave it to him.

Dad had a particular fondness for Southern Baptist missionaries and provided them free dental services. Later on, he led a Southern Baptist world missions group. I'm not sure what that entailed, but I know he didn't travel overseas.

The stories of the missionaries and Dad's obvious reverence for them emboldened me, and I took seriously my duty to spread the gospel of Christ. I decided the souls most in need of saving were those of my Jewish grandparents.

At their next visit to Danville, while Grandpa Herman was polishing off his "medicine" and after Grandma Sadye had retired to her room, I brought out my white leatherette Bible with my name inscribed on the front in gold letters. I intended to inform him of the precarious state of his immortal soul.

"Grandpa," I said. "I want to talk to you about something important, because I love you very much."

"Go ahead," he replied.

I did not know how to gracefully get into the subject, so I decided to walk the plank and take the plunge.

"Grandpa, unless you accept Jesus as your savior, you'll go to hell when you die."

He located something fascinating at the bottom of his "medicine."

"You must be saved," I soldiered on. "And Jesus can do it, if you just take him into your heart. I love you and I want you to be saved."

Ominous silence. I was getting desperate and filled the palpable vacuum. "Grandpa, it's easy. All you have to do is believe, and Jesus will forgive all your sins."

Still no reply.

"Don't you want to go to heaven? Don't you want to be saved?"

"I'm okay just the way I am." He frowned, and his little mustache drooped at the corners. "Your grandmother has done a lot of charity work, and if anyone deserves to go to heaven, it's she."

He looked as stiff as the antlered buck's head hanging above his chair, the one that Dad shot on one of his hunting trips.

"But Grandpa," I pleaded. "Good works alone won't get you into heaven. You have to accept Jesus into your heart." I was sweating, and the Bible shook in my hands.

"And what makes you think you have all the answers?" came his chilly reply. There was an interminable silence before he walked out of the room, still clutching his glass of "medicine." I went to my room, crawled under the bedcovers, and wept, aching for his love, feeling that mine had been rejected. I also thought maybe I had screwed up and insulted Grandpa. I worried that he would hold it against me and not speak to me, like Mom did when she was mad.

After my cry, I reported my attempt at witnessing for Jesus to my parents, and my mother said, "Well, what did you expect?" Dad shrugged.

The next morning, as Grandpa and Grandma were enjoying their breakfast of dark bread and kippers, while we ate bacon and eggs, he behaved as if nothing had happened. If he harbored any resentment, he didn't show it, and I was happy and relieved. He would never mention it again, and I would write a letter after I left home and left my beliefs and apologize to him for my actions that night, for being so disrespectful of his heritage.

## 8

Mom was busy with my siblings. Dad was busy with his growing practice and his civic duties in the evenings, the Sertoma Club and the Masons. Since no one paid me much mind, I enjoyed a secret life in our basement rec room. There, I could be anyone I dreamed of being—at given times an opera singer, a dancer, a horseback rider, a concert pianist—even a blonde. If my parents wondered what I did there, they never asked.

The North Danville basement rec room had cinderblock walls painted the color of cream and a cream-and-green-streaked linoleum tile floor. It smelled musty, and the light was dim. Old wooden bookshelves lined the walls and held classical music LPs and art books—gifts and hand-me-downs from Grandpa Herman. They were not so much forbidden fruit as they were fruit left to molder in the damp basement. We didn't have bookshelves upstairs, and I don't recall seeing any reading material in the house other than copies of *Reader's Digest*, the Bible, and *Guideposts*—a magazine devoted to "faith and inspiration." Later, we had a set of encyclopedias that I consulted often when doing homework. I made an attempt to read the encyclopedia through from A to Z, but gave up around F.

Grandpa Herman's beautiful art books—containing some of the most famous paintings in history that were printed to be "suitable for framing"—were part of what drew me to the rec room. I pored over these prints, turning the pages slowly and carefully, examining each image. Pinkie and Blue Boy were my favorites, in an idealized state of young adulthood, painted by different artists at different times but linked together like Romeo and Juliet. But I didn't know the details then, I was simply taken with their beauty and their clothes.

More than once, I filched my mother's white half-slip from her bureau drawer, snuck down to the rec room, snugged the waistband around my head, and pretended I had long blonde hair. Blonde hair was important to being accepted, sought after. My hair was dark brown, and I yearned to look like Goddess Crystal in my books, *The Adventures of Idabell and Wakefield*. Though I was past reading those children's books, the image of the mermaid in the translucent white gown with flowing blonde curls stayed with me. In Mom's white half-slip, I morphed into Goddess Crystal, but a goddess with legs who could dance and swing that blonde hair around.

I played the classical music records Grandpa Herman had given us on an old portable turntable, first as an accompaniment to my dance moves. Later, I would lose the half-slip and choreograph my dance moves to the swoony feelings I had while listening to Tchaikovsky's Piano Concerto No. 1, Chopin études, and Rachmaninoff's Second Piano Concerto. The music touched my soul like nothing else did. I loved it not only because of how it made me feel, but also because it was my secret joy, and no one could make fun of me for it.

In the rec room, I belted out songs from the musical *South Pacific*, accompanying the singers on the record album. I saw the 1958 film when I was ten and—from listening endlessly to the recording—knew all the lyrics by heart. The one song that stuck with me was "You've Got to Be Carefully Taught."

I was entranced by the film's forbidden love between

Lt. Joseph Cable and a Tonkinese woman, Liat. I pulled for them to be together, despite their differences in race and background, and despite Cable's own resistance. In the end, Cable dies on his secret mission, and Liat never sees him again. I was so pained by the death of Cable and the relationship, that the lyrics haunted me.

They awakened me to the understanding that bigotry was not normal. It was learned. There was no legitimate reason why Liat and Lt. Cable shouldn't be together.

I didn't know it then, but Rogers and Hammerstein's lyrics were groundbreaking and controversial. When the show was on tour in the South, Georgia lawmakers introduced a bill outlawing entertainment with "communist" overtones. One legislator went so far as to say that a song justifying interracial marriage was "a threat to the American Way of Life."

The basement also harbored Dad's collection of medical textbooks. He was originally a pre-med student but decided on dentistry to shorten the length of his training; he had a wife and children to support. These books were all shelved together in a small corner of the basement. My curiosity got the better of me, and I began leafing through the textbooks and found real photos of patients with all manner of diseases, black squares blanking out the faces on the naked bodies. There were rashes and boils and hugely swollen ankles. Rather than being repulsed by what I saw, I was fascinated. I also felt I was getting away with something smutty. Looking at naked bodies would have been forbidden, had my parents known. But they didn't. In the basement, I was free to follow my curiosity wherever it led.

## 9

As I was entering fifth grade, Dad took a flight to New York City. He offered no explanation, and Mom said, "Daddy's going to have minor surgery."

"Why? What for?" I asked, more than a little concerned.

"You know how he snores at night." Well, yes I did. Sometimes the whole house rattled. "His deviated septum causes it—that thing in the middle of the nose. His cousin's going to fix it, so Daddy will be able to breathe better."

Cousin? I'd never heard about a cousin in New York. "Who's this cousin you're talking about?"

"He's the plastic surgeon who'll do the operation."

"Is it dangerous?"

"No, it's routine, and Daddy will only be gone about a week."

"But why does he have to go so far away to have the surgery? Can't he have it done here?" There was something cloak and dagger about this abrupt trip.

"It's all settled," Mom said. "His cousin will do the surgery almost for free."

I guessed this made sense, but I still thought it was fishy. Something in the way my mother talked about it—a little too slick, which was not like her.

We drove to the Danville airport to pick him up. I was prepared to rush up and hug him, telling him how much we'd missed him. But when he descended the steps of the airliner to the tarmac, I couldn't budge. I

*Younger professional Hugh at left and older post-nose-job Hugh at right.*

didn't recognize him. Mom went up to him and took his arm as if everything was normal. It wasn't. Dad left for New York with a face I knew and loved. He came home to Danville a stranger. He'd had more than a surgery for a deviated septum. He'd had a nose job.

I couldn't bring myself to embrace him. His face was different. The full mouth was still there, but his nose looked shorter, wider, the nostrils more prominent. To me, he had always been handsome and invincible. Now, he seemed vulnerable. What that vulnerability was, I couldn't define, but I sensed it. I felt a hot shock of betrayal. If he had asked my opinion, I would have insisted he stay the same. It took days for me to warm up to him, and I never liked the new nose.

## 10

Throughout my childhood, I watched Dad bring home wild game from his weekend hunting trips—deer, duck, rabbit, and quail. He had hunted in upstate New York as a teenager, so he wasn't new to the sport, but I'm certain he didn't inherit his affinity for shooting things in the woods from Grandpa Herman.

Dad took pleasure in the gruff camaraderie of his beer-swilling hunting cronies. Being part of this club required things like chewing tobacco, having the right hunting dogs, wearing camouflage jackets and hats with flaps, and not shaving. They'd go off for long weekends of buddying around in the woods with their shotguns. Dad would return with three-days' growth of beard, which made the hair on his chin almost as long as the hair on his crew-cut head, and with a few inches lopped off the tail of his plaid flannel shirt.

It was customary to lose a shirttail if you shot at and missed a buck—a symbolic emasculation that my father bore with a sheepish grin. To prove that he'd made the grade, Dad had the head of a buck he'd killed stuffed and mounted and staring from the knotty pine wall of our den. It was opposite the glistening body of a large rainbow trout trophy. I referred to the buck as the "poor deer departed."

Dad seemed more at home with the men at the country store than with the men of his business and professional class, though he could talk to a tree stump if

necessary. He never met a stranger. He appeared to enjoy the company of these old farmers, because they accepted him, even looked up to him. I sometimes accompanied Dad on his weekend outings to Curtis Hanks's
country store, though I was bored and fidgety at these
gatherings. I went because he wanted me to go, and I
would do anything to please him. My siblings didn't go,
though my brother may have when he got older. I usually was the only kid—and the only female—there. Dad
sat reared back on two legs of an old wooden chair, trading stories with the locals, who called him Doc. "Doc, I
heard them blues was runnin' at the coast. You plannin'
on goin' out there to catch a mess of 'em?"

"You bet, Earl." Dad spat a black stream of tobacco
juice into a tin can he was holding at his knee. "Just as
soon as I get the Chevy tuned up."

Though he could talk a good line, Dad hadn't quite
mastered the art of targeted tobacco spitting. Sometimes
the juice dribbled down his chin before it reached the
can. I thought it gross beyond belief that Dad, a dentist, would be seen in public with dark commas of tobacco spittle at the corners of his mouth, unlike Grandpa
Herman's talking corners. I reminded him that he was
just a rank amateur compared to Uncle Ranny, an old
relative on my mother's side who lived in a farmhouse
outside Chapel Hill. Uncle Ranny could nail a copper
spittoon from ten paces.

Dad compelled us to eat what he killed, happy that
he could put wild game on the table. My mother cooked
the meat that Dad skinned and quartered, though she
didn't know much about how to prepare it to get the
gaminess out. During those dinners, my teeth occasionally cracked down on a piece of buckshot lodged deep in
the meat, and I protested. My pacifist nature recoiled at
eating what had met such a violent end at the hands of

my father. "Eat up," he said, sounding exasperated. "At least it's not roadkill."

The wild duck he brought home once was the limit. It must've spoiled before my mother cooked it, and the smell lingered in the house for hours. None of us had much of an appetite for whatever was substituted that night.

In November of 1960, *The Bee*, Danville's afternoon paper, celebrated Dad's hunting prowess with a photo of him in his hunting gear, crouched beside the ten-point buck he bagged with a twelve-gauge shotgun, the first buck of the season. Dad obligingly held up the dead animal's head to show its glorious rack to the photographer. I'd rather have seen the rack on a live buck. He already had one buck mounted on the wall. I didn't understand why he would need another. I was not proud of my father's hunting exploits.

Those hands that skinned and cut up wild game were the same ones that wielded a drill, a probe, or a pair of extractors back at his dental office on Monday mornings. Dad was best known for his meticulous crown and bridge work and for being able to tell a great joke while hunched over the gaping mouth of a helpless patient, drilling out a cavity or shaping a tooth to receive its porcelain or gold crown. He whistled tunes and made up funny lyrics to old songs: "I dream of Jeannie with the light green skin" or "fangs for the memories." His patients loved it.

෧෧෧෧෧

As Dad's practice prospered, we moved to increasingly nicer and larger houses, except for one detour to a garage apartment when I was nine. Dad had decided the best way to live in our dream home would be for him to contract it and have it built, so he bought a lot with a garage apartment—literally a couple of rooms behind two garage doors with a bathroom and a tiny kitchen, an apartment created in what normally would be only a garage. The plan was to add the house onto the garage and be there to supervise the building process.

Once some of our stuff was stored and the rest loaded into the apartment, boxes stacked upon boxes, my mother sat in the middle of the concrete floor and cried. She didn't have Dad's optimism, nor his grand, long-term vision, and neither did I. My mother had my sympathy. Moving a family of five (my youngest sister had not yet made her appearance) was overwhelming, especially when you had to do it so often and especially into a glorified garage with a couple of sinks.

Since Mom appeared rooted to the floor, unable to function, I began opening boxes, taking out the kitchen items first, while my younger two siblings jumped on the beds that were jammed up against the garage doors. At least they're having fun, I thought.

I'm not sure we ever completely unpacked. Our stay in the apartment was short-lived. After tearful entreaties from Mom, Dad conceded defeat and rented a brick house on Norwood Drive in North Danville. It was to be a temporary abode until Dad could find his way back to building the house he wanted.

The opportunity came when a new, upscale neighborhood, Windsor Heights, sprouted just outside town. Dad bought a lot and hired a contractor to build a brick rancher big enough for our family of six—my youngest sister, Jane, having recently made her debut when Mom was forty-two.

The move to Windsor Heights signaled that Dad had arrived. We had joined the business and professional classes who lived south of the river. But Windsor Heights was for new money, like the managers who moved down from the North to run the Goodyear and Corning plants that had sprung up. That was probably a good thing for us—no old-line Virginia families to have to contend with. And Windsor Heights had no covenants preventing Jews from living there.

We weren't Jews, but Dad hadn't been able to camouflage himself to blend in the way he did when he went hunting. I begged him to join the country club so I could use the swimming pool, but he always refused. I don't think it was about the money. It was more about the fear of being rejected by the club, but I didn't know it then. I simply felt deprived of the things my friends enjoyed. I had learned that nagging would get me nowhere. Dad was deaf to nagging.

I discovered early on that Southerners place a high value on a person's roots and sense of place. New acquaintances would inevitably ask about our last name. "Kossoff," they'd say, as if biting into some exotic fruit. "That's an unusual name. Where y'all from?"

Since my Jewish and Southern Baptist roots grew family trees as different as a magnolia and a Douglas fir, this presented a problem, which I usually resolved by shrugging and saying, "I'm from here, just like you." But the effect of these questions on me was a feeling of being different, of not being good enough.

In Sunday school, my teacher, Mrs. Calhoun, once asked, "Jean, why don't you explain the Jewish holidays to the rest of the students?"

Taken off guard, I blurted, "How would I know? I'm Baptist like you."

She did a quick pivot and said, "Okay, then. Let's talk about the meaning of Easter and why it's the most sacred holiday for Christians."

Our new house at 194 Fairmont Circle in Windsor Heights had four bedrooms, two baths, a knotty-pine-paneled den, a formal living room, an eat-in kitchen, a formal dining room, and a finished basement, not to mention the "breezeway"—a screened patio connecting the house and the carport. The living room, with its four-seater sofa and high-backed chairs with needlepoint floral designs, was off-limits. There was a halo around that room, which was strictly for show and for guests. Most often those guests were people from the church, including the minister and his wife. By that time, we were attending "high Baptist" West Main Baptist Church with a PhD minister, Dr. Lee. Dad was a deacon. He had proved his Baptist *bona fides* by helping found North Main Baptist Church in North Danville when we lived there.

Early on in Windsor Heights, when there were few other homes and even fewer kids my age to play with, I spent a couple of summers doing nothing but reading, and when I couldn't stare at another paragraph, I rode my blue Lady Schwinn around the neighborhood streets. Sometimes I climbed the hill across the highway and threw dirt clods onto cars passing below—or hunted crawdads in the stream nearby. I was lonely.

Mine was not the era when kids were carpooled to sports activities or art classes or specialized camps. I was on my own.

I sighed at the prospect of this everyday routine

dragging on through the summer. I thought of how Grandpa Herman had promised to take me with him to Europe. I could be doing exciting things with him instead of withering in the airless summer heat of a small town, nearly dying of boredom. It was then that I latched onto the idea of getting out of that terminally stuffy town as soon as I was able. Life had to be more exciting in big cities like New York, where Dad had wandered unsupervised when he was a boy.

Picking on my siblings helped while away the time. I especially relished scaring the beejezus out of them by telling them ghost stories. In summer, after dinner, I gathered them, and any other gullible young neighborhood kids I could commandeer, at the nearest new home construction site. We would find a safe but secluded spot amongst the bricks and boards and sit in a circle. The smell of fresh cut timber wafted by, and fireflies traced their neon-mating dance in the distance. As I neared the scariest bits, I could hear the sharp intake of a chorus of breaths. In the lowering darkness, I could see how wide the several sets of eyes were. This gave me great satisfaction, until Mom called us home and scolded me.

"Jean, how many times have I told you not to go near those construction sites? It's dangerous, especially at night. You could have gotten your brother and sister seriously injured."

The hint of danger excited me. I was my father's daughter, and Dad seemed afraid of nothing.

We siblings fought, though I only remember fighting with my brother. He was the only son and Dad's chosen; he had what I considered the lion's share of attention and lighter chores—like clipping grass outside or taking out the garbage. He was spared the hours of ironing sheets and my father's boxer shorts—a task I thought silly, since we'd only be lying on the sheets, and no one would see Dad's boxers but himself. My mother supervised these tasks, making me go over a wrinkle that might have escaped my notice. "If a job's worth doing, it's worth doing right," she insisted, while I thought that the job wasn't worth doing to begin with.

I have no memory of what caused my brother and me to fight, sometimes in hand-to-hand combat, but I suspect I was jealous. By then, Dad spent more of his free time with my brother, hunting and fishing. In response, I developed feelings of not being good enough to get Dad's attention. If I were only prettier or smarter, maybe Dad would play checkers with me the way he used to.

My mother, like most Southern mothers, coddled the only boy. When Mom arrived red-faced to break up a fight, my brother usually claimed victimhood, because "Jean scratched me with her fingernails." Occasionally that was true. Mom sent us to our rooms or, if she was mad enough, made me go out and cut a switch while my brother got off with a reprimand.

My sisters and I called my brother "the Jewish prince" behind his back, because he was always getting a break and was not held to the same standard as we girls. My brother had the dual blessing of being the Jewish prince as well as the Southern coddled boy. After all, it was his sacred duty to find a profession, procreate, and pass on the family name. We would just be somebody's wives.

We all got switchings at one time or another. Like my siblings, I had to go outside, locate, and cut the switch that would deliver the punishment. If I came back with a puny one, my mother sent me out again to find one that could inflict welts. You weren't well and truly punished until you had a few welts on your legs. If more urgency was called for, a flyswatter or hairbrush would do. The physical punishment was often accompanied by a lecture as Mom invoked the words, "Let that be a lesson to you."

The switchings and the lectures only made me mad. The one time my mother slapped me in the face for mouthing off at her, I stormed off to my room, seething with hatred. I was thirteen at the time. I don't remember what I said, only that it was disrespectful and I was in her face. I do remember that she talked to the minister at our church about me.

Following that church consultation, my mother sat me down and with her stern Southern Baptist face on, began, "It says in the Bible that you are to honor your father and your mother. When you talk back like that, you are breaking God's word." With that admonition, she jabbed a finger just shy of my face. "As long as you live under my roof, you will be respectful and you will be obedient, do you hear me?"

"Yes, I hear you."

I heard her with a mixture of contrition and rebellion. The contrition won out.

"I'm sorry, Mom." But really, had I gone through the trials of baptism for this?

Dad was no help, since he always backed up Mom. He was too busy to pay me much attention. He had the son he'd always wanted. I was pushed to the periphery.

I tried to clean up my act. The best way to do that was to hive off in my room, or in the basement. I spent my time reading, doing homework, listening to music, and avoiding my family. Throughout junior high and high school, I kept to myself. Being seen and not heard was good but being not seen and not heard was better.

❦❦❦❦❦

Some of our fighting, mostly my brother's and mine, was over resources that should have been abundant but were, for some unknown reason, in short supply, especially at the dinner table. There was a tight race to see who could get the last slice of roast beef or boiled potato, sometimes with forks dueling in mid-air. I knew we had plenty of money for food. I didn't understand why Mom just didn't make more of it.

Dad usually finished his meal before the rest of us had barely begun. "I'm still on army time," he announced. If he inhaled his food, it was because of the habits he acquired as an airman. Sometimes he left the table to work on something in the garage. Sometimes he stayed.

I wondered if his obsession with turning off the lights was army-inspired too. He wasn't normally a man who nagged, but he carped about wasting electricity when one of us left a light on. Flossing our teeth nightly was right up there with saving electricity. Lord knows, if I didn't floss, mysterious bacteria would spend the night between my teeth and begin digging a cavity. Dad being my dentist turned me into a fervent flosser. There was nothing I was more afraid of than having Dad fill a cavity.

"This is such a small one, you won't need Novocaine," Dad said more than once, as he ignored my shrieks of pain when the drill went in and hit a nerve. Surely he didn't treat other kids that way—kids who weren't his own. I thought he had a mean streak when it came to working on my teeth, though I never told him so. Talking back to Dad never got me anywhere. It provoked ominous silence, and next time might be worse. The other thing he liked to do was squeeze my knee between his thumb and the rest of his fingers at just the right spot to hit a nerve. He relented only when I squealed, "Stop, Dad, you're hurting me."

Our family dinners were jokey affairs and generally featured Dad as the butt of the hilarity. He seemed to invite it. If we weren't giggling at his choice of slouchy, down-at-the-heel clothes or his hunting buddies, we were teasing him about his use of Yiddish words.

"Say, Dad, what's the difference between a *schmuck*, a *schmendrick*, and a *schlemiel*?"

He had used those words often when referring to some jerk he had run across.

"Well, a *schmendrick* and a *schlemiel* are roughly the same thing," Dad explained. "*Schmendricks* are dumb, bumbling guys working up to being *schlemiels*, who are even worse. But a *schmuck*, he's different."

"How Dad? You call people schmucks all the time."

"That's because they deserve it. I reserve *schmuck* for the worst of the worst."

"But what is a *schmuck*, Dad?"

My mother gave Dad "the look."

"I'll tell you some other time," he answered. "Just don't use that word yourselves."

*Schmuck*, I found out, is the old Yiddish word for penis. I liked the word and saying it felt good, but not within my parents' earshot. Dad would have been okay with it, but Mom, definitely not.

The first time I used the word "lie," Mom jumped on me as if I'd whacked my brother. "We don't use the word 'lie.' We say 'he or she told a story.'" We kids were forbidden to use any cuss words, but Mom had substitutions like: "Oh, fathers; oh, sugar; son of a gun."

I preferred Dad's Yiddish insults, especially *schmuck*, or if I wanted to be sarcastic, exclaiming *oi vey*, which was actually meant to express dismay or exasperation. I loved the sound of it, the feeling of those rounded vowels in my mouth.

⁂⁂⁂⁂⁂

Now that we were attending a high Baptist church, Mom felt it was important to entertain and frequently held dinners for various West Main church members. The first to be invited were the minister Dr. Lee and his wife. My mother was proud of her role as the "wife of a professional man," a phrase she used often to explain why she had to look good when going out and why we had to have a pristine living room for guests.

That night, she took special care with the table setting—instructing me which china to use and what drinking glasses to place where. There were flowers in the center of the table, set for five. Being included at the grown-up table was a source of pride, and I happily obeyed my mother's instructions. The younger kids ate in the kitchen. The main course of roast beef and potatoes went over well. Conversation stayed on track. (With Dad, you could never be sure of that.) I was on my best behavior.

Then it was time for dessert and coffee. As I helped clear the table, Dad motioned for Dr. Lee to follow him into the den to listen to a record he had just bought. Dad thought this record was hilarious and wanted to share his discovery with Dr. Lee, though he was mum about the record's content. He wanted it to be a surprise. Mom knew what was up.

"Hugh," she said with that slightly imperious tone she sometimes used with me, one that was guaranteed to provoke deafness in Dad. "We're about to serve dessert. Save that for another time."

But Dad had already pushed back from the table and was not about to sit down again.

Mom soldiered on, making conversation with Mrs. Lee during the performance in the adjacent room. I already had heard the recording—of farting sounds. There was the "triple flutter buster," with accompanying sound effects, as well as the "toot'n flute" and the "trouser trumpet." I could hear Dad guffawing, but not much from Dr. Lee.

The "double bubble boomer" was the last straw. Mom had been progressively getting redder in the face and finally excused herself. She pushed back from the table and went to fetch Dad and drag him in by the collar, if necessary.

At the door to the den, Mom said, "Hugh, turn that thing off and come back to the dining room." The men returned, and my mother served dessert, but the table conversation never recovered.

It seemed to me that Dad had trouble separating his good ol' boy persona from his professional man persona. The good ol' boy had risen ascendant during the formal dinner with the minister and his wife, which had required more of a "professional man."

I wondered if he enjoyed embarrassing Mom, because she put so much stock in being "the wife of a professional man." While I, too, thought Dad's after-dinner entertainment was inappropriate, I was amused at the show. Watching the scene play out was like seeing a comedy skit. But I kept my face neutral and my feelings to myself.

❦❦❦❦❦

The downside of moving to Windsor Heights was I had to change schools. I began sixth grade at Forest Hills Elementary, the school that served the children of Danville's old money, many of whom lived in Forest Hills, the city's toniest neighborhood. The less reverent of us called the denizens of Forest Hills FFVs—short for first families of Virginia.

The streets of Forest Hills were laid out like the spokes of a wheel coming off one central hub. All the streets radiating from that hub were named Hawthorne, confusing anyone who ventured in and didn't belong. Black maids and gardeners could come and go, as long as they kept to their service roles.

At Forest Hills Elementary, the other kids ignored me as if I were the gum on the bottoms of their shoes. My past in North Danville and my status as the new kid in school dragged on me like a pair of leg irons, and I was miserable. Until then, I had attended schools in North Danville and had been a star student, the center of my social group. I had attended three different grammar schools before Forest Hills and I had a knack for fitting in quickly—or so I thought. But my feelings of not being good enough came to the fore when I started Forest Hills. I remember being terrified of reciting a poem or reading a book passage in front of the class. On such occasions when the teacher called on me, my heart thrummed, my knees knocked, and my hands shook. I sweated and I could barely rasp out the words that felt like hot pokers in my mouth. I was humiliated. All I wanted was to disappear.

I was so unhappy that I feigned illness to avoid having to go to school—me, the hearty, enthusiastic straight-A student. My parents soon caught on. They sent me to school unless I could prove I was sick by running a fever. I was sick, though—heartsick, lonely, and excluded. The one student who befriended me was Melody Malone, a soft-eyed girl with brown curls, because she had transferred to Forest Hills a year earlier and knew what it felt like.

I became withdrawn and listless. An alien displaced the outgoing, happy tomboy I had been and substituted a sad, painfully shy person, all confidence gone. If I was predisposed to feel that I was not good enough, Forest Hills Elementary proved to me that I was right. Not being good enough would become a permanent part of the story I told myself and would follow me through the years and the challenges to come.

For relief from my profound shyness, I found consolation in books. I read in my room or on the old avocado-green sofa in the basement rec room. My first literary crush was Charles Dickens's *David Copperfield*. I loved David, because he suffered abuse by a cruel stepfather and remained a kind soul who stood up for fat Tommy Traddles, a boy mercilessly bullied at Salem House School. I was hooked on Dickens. Next came *A Tale of Two Cities*, followed by *Great Expectations* and *Oliver Twist*. Dickens was my entertainer and my savior. His characters, the good ones, were my friends and role models. When I was reading a Dickens book, I entered completely into that world, like a time traveler. I also devoured James Michener's *Tales of the South Pacific* and *Hawaii*, which fueled my desire for travel and adventure.

If my childhood was bound by religious fundamentalism and small-town pettiness, I could roam the world and see intimately into the lives of others through books. Someday, I vowed, I would see the world myself.

## 12

Often after Sunday church services and our midday meal at Mary's Diner, Dad drove the back roads of Pittsylvania County looking for farm property.

One Sunday, we wound up behind a dark green Chevy pickup truck with a full gun rack and Confederate flag sticker on the back window. We saw the backs of two heads. There were other pickups, sedans, and muscle cars lined up behind us, as if we accidently had become part of a parade.

"I bet a Klan rally just broke up," Dad said, adding one of his favorite epithets, "crumb bums."

The pickup ahead pulled into the passing lane and we could see that an old battered car had been in front of it. Instead of passing, the truck edged toward the old car as if it was going to nudge the vehicle over.

"Look what they're doing," Dad said. "They're trying to run those colored people off the road."

Which is what they did. The old car moved onto the shoulder of the road to avoid being sideswiped. The gun-toting truck sped off. The guy in the truck's passenger seat had his window rolled down and yelled something. His arm and hand were outside the window with his middle finger up.

"*Schmucks*," Dad muttered as he slowed our car to let the car on the roadside back into the line of traffic.

"It's awful," Mom said.

"Can't we do anything, Dad?" I asked.

"No, it would only make things worse, especially with a line of those clowns behind us."

I worried that another of those clowns would try to run the old car off the road again. The scene I'd witnessed both puzzled and frightened me. I didn't know much about the Klan, but I knew they were not good people. What might those Klan members do to me or to Dad if we crossed paths? After all, my father was a Jew by birth.

Dad was the only dentist in Danville who treated black patients, usually for free, but he scheduled them first thing in the morning or last thing in the evening so they did not cross paths with his white patients. He said, "If the white patients knew I was treating coloreds, I'd lose my practice." I was proud of Dad for taking that risk, but I also was angry that white people could be so ignorant. In our house, I rarely heard a racist comment, except for my mother occasionally referring to blacks as "darkies." The preferred term at the time was "colored people."

When I was a young girl, I did not identify Danville's white-only bathrooms, separate water fountains, separate restaurants, and limiting colored people to the upper gallery of the movie theater as racist. It was the norm, and I didn't question it—until Cora entered our lives.

Cora Patterson became part of our family after the move to Windsor Heights. Cora was the daughter of a sharecropper, and she needed work. My mother was only too happy to hire someone to shoulder a chunk of the daily drudgery of housework and cooking. Our first black maid, Dorothy, had become indispensable when we lived in North Danville. She was kind and reliable, and I liked her. When Dorothy left, and we subsequently moved to Windsor Heights, Mom was desperate for help.

I was twelve and Cora eighteen at the time. She lived with her parents in Martinsville, Virginia, thirty miles northwest of Danville. The daily commute would have been too much, so she moved in and spent her weekdays with us, returning to her family on weekends. She ate meals at our table and watched TV with us in the evenings. Dad added a pine-paneled bedroom off the rec room in the basement where Cora slept and kept her things. She had her own half-bath adjacent to the bedroom.

At the time, I didn't recognize how unusual it was to have the hired help be a part of the family. Dad was egalitarian in an era when race and class distinctions were tightly woven into the fabric of our community. He was conscious of his status in town. He got on the board of this and was president of that, but he seemed more comfortable around his less-educated hunting and fishing buddies who took him at face value, as a friend, and even looked up to him. Dad's public face was separate from the private one. Was the duality an issue, difficult to maintain? I don't know.

Cora was pretty, I thought, and I relished the feel of her velvet-soft skin when I kissed her cheek. I loved her smile and her beautiful straight, white teeth. My own had a gap in the front, so I had to wear a retainer to close it.

I adored Cora as the older sister I never had and as the mother whose love I was missing. I loved her with a devotion I lavished on no one else. When I came home hungry from school, she cooked up the world's most mouth-watering cinnamon rolls or her special homemade French fries. As a teenager, I was always hungry.

I sat at the kitchen table and watched Cora slice potatoes and throw them into the deep fryer. As she worked, we discussed my day at school, my most recent crush, or the latest school gossip. As soon as the fries were crisp and had filled the kitchen with an aroma that made me drool, she resurrected them from the fryer and dumped the lot in a brown paper bag, which she shook to absorb the extra grease. Cora's fries set a standard that other fries anywhere else or anytime later could never meet.

It was a time when girls set their hair on rollers, sometimes the size of coffee cans, and backcombed it to achieve an extra few inches of height—to sport the bouffant or the beehive. You had to sleep in the curlers overnight to get the desired look. The effect on sleep was like trying to drift off with your head nestled in a bed of rocks.

Cora was my collaborator and my biggest supporter in all things to do with appearance. She understood the importance of wrestling my natural waves into smooth submission so I could look like the other girls in my classes. On hair washing nights, I sat on a chair in my room, towel draped around my shoulders, while Cora carefully sectioned off rows of wet hair and set each section on pink sponge rollers. She had much more patience for it than I, and she brushed it out the next morning and helped me backcomb it. My bouffant gave my head a certain light bulb shape.

When she was setting my hair, Cora and I talked about boys and sex. Sometimes, like the teenagers we both were, we'd lie across my bed and share secrets.

"I'm in love with my history teacher, Mr. Caldwell," I confided. "When I'm in class, I can't take my eyes off his chest in his white shirt with the button-down collar. All I want to do is lay my head on that chest. Is that weird?"

"Not a bit. I've done way more than that with a man."

"No, Cora, did you go all the way?"

Cora was silent but nodded an affirmative.

"Wow. What's it like? I mean, I know the details now, but I don't know if it hurts, especially at first. It must feel good, since people keep doing it."

"Yep, pretty good. Now listen," she said. "I'm gonna tell you how you can fool a man into thinking he's having sex with you."

I was at attention.

"The first thing you do is grease up your hand real good with some lotion. Then you hold that greased-up hand between your legs and let him put his thing in there and go at it."

I was skeptical. "But won't he know he's in your hand and not in you?"

"Nah," she replied. "He'll be so het up he won't notice the difference. I've done it myself several times."

"Wow," was all I could reply. I didn't allow my face to reflect the shock I felt at her advice.

Cora was a pro at more practical things, too. She taught me how to get a window spotless with just vinegar and old newspaper and how to season a mess of collard greens with just the right amount of fatback. When I didn't make the high school cheerleading squad, she comforted me.

Every morning before school, I presented myself for her inspection. One morning, I had on a white blouse with a Peter Pan collar and a silver-toned circle pin, tucked into a tan pleated skirt. "You'd better ease off those cinnamon rolls," she said, laughing. "You don't want those hips to grow too much more."

Cora's jest got me to worrying about all those French fries I was eating after school and what they might be adding to my hips.

"But, does this look okay?" I begged, forever seeking her approval.

"You look just fine," she said. "Now go on off to school, because I got work to do."

I have no memory of what my mother was doing when Cora was sending me to school. Maybe she was tending to the younger ones. At the time, my world was all about me, so I was focused on Cora because she was there for me when my mother was not.

❧❧❧❧❧

Cora always accompanied us on our family vacations, even though she had an aversion to the beach, because the sun would darken her skin. She was there to cook and clean. It wasn't a vacation for her.

Nags Head, on the Outer Banks of North Carolina, was our favorite vacation destination when I was in grammar school. The trip was the highlight of my year. To deal with my nervous impatience on departure day, I ran circles around the house and then pumped myself up on the old metal swing as high as I could go. Dad had the unenviable job of squeezing all our suitcases, the fishing gear, the beach toys, the extra towels, and the games into the rear of Bullet—not to mention making room for the cat carrier containing our gray cat, Fuzzy. Dad tied the overflow to the luggage rack on top of the car, and he threatened more than once to put Fuzzy up there—as a joke that I didn't see the humor in.

Mom was concerned that we all have on clean underwear for the trip, in case we had an accident and had to go to a hospital. What would strangers think of us if they discovered dirty underwear while trying to save our lives?

The year I was twelve, I had a brand new white Naugahyde suitcase, of which I was inordinately proud. Finally, I didn't have to share an old suitcase with my sister. I thought the blue silk-like lining with pockets was beautiful and elegant, and I carefully packed it the way Cora taught me, rolling each item of clothing in a neat package so that I could fit more in—two swimsuits, shorts, tops, panties, my trainer bra, beach towel, flip flops, a hairbrush, and a toothbrush. As I watched Dad pack the car, I spotted my new suitcase being strapped to the luggage rack on top.

"No, no, Dad," I wailed. "Please put it in the back of the car. If you put my suitcase on top, it'll get wet if it rains."

"It's not going to rain," Dad said. "Stop kvetching and get in the car."

"But you could switch out my suitcase with something in the back."

"I'm done with the packing, so that's the end of it. Get in the car or we'll leave without you."

I didn't argue further because it would be useless, plus I wanted a window seat in the back.

Well, it rained on that trip—we went through a summer thunderstorm. When we arrived at the cottage, and Dad had taken the overflow off the top of the wagon, I grabbed my suitcase, dragged it onto the porch, and opened it. Ugly brown water stains had dripped down the blue lining. I pulled out my favorite yellow shorts and the sleeveless top with the daises. They were damp and smelled funny. I was mad and self-righteous. Having been proven right was no comfort.

"See, I told you what would happen, and it did," I whined when Dad opened the screen door to the porch. "You ruined my new suitcase."

"Pipe down about that suitcase," Dad said, scowling. He didn't say, "shut up," because Mom said those were bad words. I closed my suitcase, dragged it up the stairs into one of the bedrooms, and sulked.

That only reminded me of an earlier trip when I left my purse, containing the important love notes my grammar school crush Kenny had written me, on the back ledge of the toilet at a rest stop. Once I realized that I didn't have it with me, less than ten minutes from the time we stopped, I begged Dad to go back so I could retrieve the black patent leather purse with the daisy on the front, encased in clear plastic.

"Quit nagging about the purse. Forget it. We're not going back," Dad barked, and Mom wouldn't intervene. What a *schmuck*, I thought, but didn't say. Instead, I cried quietly, with that feeling of hopelessness that would plague me into my teenage years. Why wasn't I important enough to be listened to?

Whenever we headed toward the Outer Banks, Dad drove like a wild man. Truckers were his favorite fellow drivers. He loved to hand signal the big rig drivers roaring by in the opposite direction. "Rev it up" involved an upward spiraling motion of the forefinger. A flicking of headlights meant, "Cop ahead."

Dad was obsessed with getting from point A to point B in as little time as possible. On a two-lane highway when there were yellow dotted lines indicating he could pass, Dad floored the gas pedal to put a slowpoke in his rearview mirror, while my mother pleaded, "Don't Hugh. It's too dangerous. Think of the children."

Per usual, Dad went deaf to Mom's appeals. I figured he knew what he was doing, so I didn't get worked up like Mom did. Still, she had a point. Sometimes Dad ignored Mom as much as he ignored me.

We kids counted cars and played the license plate game. "I saw one from Georgia." Lick the finger and make a one in the air.

"I saw the one from Georgia and one from South Carolina." Two licks and two imaginary lines in the air.

"You're just making that up."

"I did so see it. Not my fault Dad passed that car."

"Look at that Burma-Shave sign!"

"HE'S THE GUY / THE GALS FORGOT / HIS STYLE / WAS SMOOTH / HIS CHIN WAS NOT," we chorused as Dad passed each separate sign.

Dad added his own version: "Only crumb bums / Wear / Facial hair."

The first time Cora went to the shore with us, we stopped at a rural restaurant for lunch. As we exited the car, I pulled Cora along with me, but she held back. What was going on?

"I'll just eat in the car," Cora said.

"No, Cora. You can eat with us inside."

Cora was silent. The others had gone into the restaurant, and Dad came back out to get me.

"I've ordered for Cora," he said.

"But why, Dad?" I asked, perplexed. "She can order for herself."

"Jean, just get inside," Dad said with exasperation.

"No, I'm not leaving Cora."

Dad shrugged, left, and returned later, saying, "Your chow's ready, Cora."

That's when Cora got out of the car, and the two of us went around to the back of the restaurant where, after the screen door opened, a hand stuck out holding a plate of food. Cora took it, and we walked back to Bullet.

"I'll take my food in the car, too," I told Dad, who was waiting by the car to see that Cora got her food.

This time he didn't push me. I was allowed to go in and get my plate when it was ready and take it to the car. It was hot inside the Chevy, and I could smell Cora's fried fish and hush puppies. We opened both doors so we could get a breeze flowing through. Then I settled in with my burger and fries with ketchup. I looked at Cora, who was dipping a hush puppy into seafood sauce.

"I'm mad that you can't eat with us inside," I told her.

"Don't worry, child," she said. "It's just the way things are."

She continued to look at her plate.

"But it's not right."

"Hush, now, and eat your lunch."

I wanted her to say more, but what else could she say, especially to a naïve young girl sheltered from so much of what she had to endure. It dawned on me that those separate water fountains and bathrooms were not normal after all and, in fact, were also unfair—and hurtful.

We ate in silence, but I was with the young black woman whom I thought of as my big sister, my substitute mother, and my best friend, all rolled into one, and that was enough for me.

❦❦❦❦❦

I caught my first fish at Oregon Inlet near Nags Head with Dad, who loved fishing as much as hunting. Fishing was one of the few things Mom liked to do at the beach. But this fishing expedition was just between Dad and me. I felt special, because it was rare to have time alone with Dad after my brother was born. We were at the end of the pier, and Dad showed me how to put a wriggling worm on a fishhook, no easy task when the slimy thing was trying to escape my fingers. Once baited, we tossed the hook, attached to a line and a rod and reel, into the briny water.

"Keep still," Dad instructed. "Wait until you feel a tug on the line and then pull up quickly to set the hook in the fish's mouth."

"Okay, Dad, but the line is moving," I said.

"That's just the swells of the waves," he replied. "You'll know when a fish bites."

I felt a tug. "Dad, Dad," I squealed. "I felt it."

"Okay," he said. "Now pull up on the rod and start reeling that baby in."

I did as instructed and brought to the surface a ridiculous looking fish that was flat, with both eyes on one side of its body.

"You caught a flounder!" Dad exclaimed. "Now I'll show you how to take it off the hook."

I realized that in order to get out the hook, I would have to grab the flounder's mouth. I fought my revulsion and pulled the hook out of the gaping fish mouth. Dad tossed the fish in our bucket. That was a proud day for me—my first ever catch to show Cora and the rest of the family.

Not content to teach me how to drop a line and reel in a fish, Dad felt I needed to see how to clean and debone a fish, too, a task I wasn't much interested in. It was bloody and slimy, and I had better things to do. But he insisted. I watched as he deftly sliced through the flounder's belly and removed its guts. Then he went after the bones, pulling out a connected set down the middle of the fish.

"I don't think I'll be doing a lot of fish cleaning," I remarked. "I'll just catch them, and you can clean them."

"Not so fast. You'll be cleaning some more fish down the line," Dad said, not willing to let me have the last word. But I always managed to be somewhere out of earshot when Dad was cleaning fish. He recruited my brother instead.

We stayed at the same big, old weathered beach house every year. Back then, the town of Nags Head on North Carolina's Outer Banks comprised only a couple of seafood restaurants, a bait and tackle shop, and a little market where you could pick up milk. After stopping for fresh milk, we arrived at our gray, shingled six-bedroom beach house. Right on the shore, the house had a jaunty nautical feel, especially the wood-paneled bedrooms at the top of a winding flight of stairs, and a big screened porch with rocking chairs that cradled me and my siblings when we came off the beach, gritty and wind-blown. We had a view of the ocean, the sand, and sea oats. The beach was pristine, the breakers impressive, and the undertow fierce. Dad took me out beyond the breakers, and we rode the swells together, me clinging to his back and screaming in delight as each new wave rose up, high as the walls of our house—or so it seemed to me then. I felt safe with Dad. He was a strong swimmer.

Whenever Dad paid attention to me, I forgot the mean and sometimes nutty things he would say and do—like in restaurants, continuously tapping his water glass with a knife to make noise that would embarrass Mom, while we waited for our food. He often did things like that to get Mom's goat.

Mom couldn't swim, and she did not like to sunbathe. She never lived down the time she got seasick on an inner tube. Instead of going in the water, Mom sat on a towel under a beach umbrella, watching my youngest sister, who was two at the time. Cora usually stayed in the cottage or in a rocking chair on the screened porch—when she wasn't sweeping up sand or making lunches and dinners. She liked to fish, so she sometimes accompanied Mom and Dad to the pier at the end of the day, when the sun was setting.

For entertainment, there were mountainous sand dunes known as Jockey's Ridge that we children climbed and then raced down, plus whatever diversions we could manufacture on our own. When the weather was bad, we turned to books, Monopoly, card games, and plays we made up and performed, using lampshades and furniture as props. At the beach, we did things together as a family and had rare fun doing so. Dad was as relaxed as he could get, which was not what most people would define as relaxed. When others were lying on the beach or drinking beer while rocking on their porches, he was either in the ocean swimming, at the pier fishing, or talking up a group of old fishermen. For us children, the rules were more relaxed, no chores or church. When the weather was good, it was heaven. When it was bad, it was still good.

## 13

Back at home, my family loved to go to movies together. When *One Hundred and One Dalmatians* opened, we were keen to see it. Even though I was twelve at the time, any chance to see a movie was a big event. Disney movies were our fare—wholesome, upbeat, and visually striking.

We all went, save for my youngest sister who was then two and staying home with Cora. We laughed and ate popcorn. Afterwards, we filed out of the theater, talking about how the main character, Cruella, was heartless, so horrible that she would kill Dalmatian pups just to create the fur coat of her dreams.

"She's evil," I said.

Dad turned to me and said with a laugh, "Hey, Cruella. Let's head to the car."

I stopped cold and couldn't speak. The name felt like a gut punch. Tears tried to push their way out, but I squeezed my eyes tight in a vain attempt to keep them from rolling down my cheeks. I wiped my face quickly with a sleeve. Being seen crying would only provoke another dig.

I had heard friends' dads addressing their daughters as Princess, Kitten, Love-Bug. There were hundreds of endearments available to dads everywhere. I had experienced no endearments from either parent. Other than the occasional Little Herman from Mom, Cruella became my first real nickname, one that Dad used until I left home.

I knew better than to ask Dad why he said that. Such a question would be fruitless and possibly draw more ridicule. It was better to accept it, so I tolerated the moniker with grim resentment.

He thought the nickname was funny. I never figured out why he called me that. Was I mean and cruel? Was it because I bossed my younger siblings—those interlopers who had pushed me off my only-child sun throne and into the outer darkness of irrelevance? I did my share of teasing and picking at them. My siblings picked up the nickname, too. Mom didn't seem to mind that Dad called me Cruella. But then, she had often compared me to Grandpa Herman, which, in her mind, was no compliment.

Only much later did it occur to me that Dad used humor and sometimes aggressive teasing to keep people at an emotional distance. Put another way, one could say that joking and teasing were his distorted ways of showing love. From the stories I heard about his childhood, I doubt he had much love growing up. What he didn't receive as a child he couldn't give to his own children.

❦❦❦❦❦ 14 ❦❦❦❦❦

Within a couple of years, Windsor Heights filled with fine houses, some in the mid-century-modern style like ours, and some traditional, like those in Forest Hills.

One of my first new friends in the neighborhood was Norma Ray Darchuk, who had moved with her family from the North so her father could take a position with Corning. Finally, another girl with a weird last name. Norma Ray wore her hair in a blonde bob with bangs, and sometimes had on lip-gloss and eye shadow. She was sophisticated and a year older than my thirteen-year-old self. I was in awe.

Norma Ray and I hung out in our basement, sitting, knees to chests, on the old green sofa, giggling about the stupid stuff our parents made us do—all their rules about girls having to do the indoor chores while boys only had to mow the lawn once a week, me having to iron the sheets and Dad's boxers. Then Norma Ray got a serious look on her face: "My mom just had a surgery on her female parts, and when she came home, she couldn't pee without screaming," she said solemnly.

"What did they do to her?" This was most distressing to hear, since I had female parts, too. I hugged my knees closer into my chest.

"I dunno for sure. Something about not having any more babies."

"But why would she need surgery to not have babies?" This was before Cora and I had our sex talks. My mother had told me nothing about the nuts and bolts of procreation, and Dad was not about to go there with me. My mother's only advice was, "Don't let boys take advantage of you." What "taking advantage of" meant, I had no idea—at least not until Norma Ray.

"You do know how babies are made, don't you?" Norma Ray shot me a look that said, "Are you serious?"

Of course I did. "From too much kissing. That's what my friend Alice told me in sixth grade."

"And you believed that?" Norma Ray rolled her eyes.

"Well, yes. A little kissing is okay, but if you kiss a lot, you'll get a baby."

"You can kiss all you want," Norma Ray laughed. "To get a baby, you have to let the man put his thing inside you."

I gulped. I knew what "the thing" was. My brother had one. But I thought it was only for peeing.

"That's disgusting," I said. "I'll never do that."

People who were married had babies, which meant they must have done the disgusting thing at least once. My parents, I reasoned, must have done it several times, since there were four of us. The thought made me nauseous. I vowed then and there to never marry.

As Windsor Heights expanded, more boys appeared along with the new houses and Norma Ray.

Some neighborhood boys were obnoxious. One of those was Paul Turner, who acted like he was superior to the rest of us. One day when I boarded the school bus, there was one empty seat, and it was beside Paul. I sat down. I was wearing my new McMullen dress, the yellow one with the butterflies on it. As soon as I sat, Paul turned in his window seat and put both feet on my thigh to push me to the floor. A lightning bolt of rage hit me. He had put his dirty shoes on my new dress, and that was too much. I punched him in the face. After school,

Paul must have gone home crying to his mommy. Mrs. Turner phoned my mother, saying that I'd given Paul a black eye. To my mother's credit, she replied, "Well, I guess he deserved it then." Paul stayed away from me after that, and I gained some new respect for my mother. When Dad got home from work, Mom told him about the scuffle, and Dad chuckled, saying, "I guess it wasn't Paul Turner's day."

When it came to anyone messing with my physical self, I had a short fuse, which didn't allow time to think about consequences. I still remember being in first grade when a boy sitting next to me tried to kiss me. I stabbed a pencil into his knee and got in trouble with the teacher. This went down in family lore as "the pencil incident."

## 15

Well into my thirteenth year, my mother came to my bedroom one day with a booklet titled, "Now You Are Thirteen." Well, yes, I thought. I wondered why she'd waited to give me the pamphlet, since I'd been thirteen for months. I was indignant that she hadn't given it to me when I turned thirteen.

Mom placed the booklet on the bed and said, "Read this, and let me know if you have any questions." Then she left the room.

I didn't know what it was about, but upon reading it, I learned, in soft colors and euphemistic terms, the details of menstruation.

Of course I didn't have any questions for Mom. If she had wanted to talk to me about such private things, she would have said something more about the booklet's contents. A few days later, she showed me the pads and sanitary belts I would have to wear when the time came, stored underneath the bathroom sink. Those were the days before self-adhesive pads. Getting trussed up with a belt with dangling clips to grab the disposable pad at each end was a complicated business. I got my period a couple of months later, near Christmas, which was about six weeks before my fourteenth birthday.

Thanks to the timely arrival of the booklet, when I started to bleed, I wasn't afraid that I was hemorrhaging or dying. I informed Mom, who showed me how to put on the loathsome sanitary belt and clip on the pad.

She said she would tell Dad, which seemed embarrassing and unnecessary. Mercifully, Dad never said anything to me, but I knew things would somehow be different. I felt a certain pride about making the transition to another stage of life but also a bigger sense of loss—of my childhood freedoms, my tomboy fun, and my relationship with Dad, who was less and less involved in my life.

⊹⊹⊹⊹⊹

In my mid-teens, Mom offered unsolicited advice about sex and marriage. I was helping her with a flower arrangement for a garden club competition, and we were alone together in the kitchen with stalks of greenery and colorful blossoms strewn around us.

We must have been talking about other things. I don't remember. It would be tough to recall anything routine after the next thing she said: "Jean, I want to tell you something that's different from what my mother told me. Something about marriage that I think you should know."

My ears pricked up, since a personal revelation from Mom was not common, and I couldn't imagine what she was about to say. She paused with a flower stalk in her hand and a pensive expression.

"My mother told me that in marriage, I would have to submit to my husband, even if there was no pleasure in it." As she said this, she was looking beyond my left ear.

I wasn't sure I wanted to hear what she was going to say. My girlfriends and Cora had already filled me in on sex.

"But I want to tell you that's not true. There can be pleasure." Mom said this as she shoved the stem of a red tulip into some ferns at the bottom of the container.

I could feel my face heat up. This territory had been off limits for as long as I had been alive. I didn't know what to say, so I kept bunching up the remaining ferns to cover more of the tulip stem. Finally, I muttered, "Okay, Mom, thanks. How about this purple Dutch iris to go along with the red?"

"That'll do," she said.

Mom had just told me something private about her and Dad. I knew it was a big moment, but it was awkward. From Mom's comments, I gathered that my parents had a healthy love life. Except for trivial things, talking to my mother had never been that easy. I simply didn't have the words to respond.

## 16

In junior high school, Cruella acquired another nickname: Teacher's Pet. Much as I tried to blend in, my bookishness gave me away. By the time I was thirteen, I had polished off most of Dickens, Dumas, Hardy, and Michener. My reputation as a literary prodigy spread beyond English class and dogged me like a social disease.

One day, Mrs. Pettigrew asked a literary question and went up and down the rows of our class, asking each student if he or she knew the answer. There were several rows of no's, and I was near the end of the line. Then a classmate blurted, "Teacher's Pet will know the answer."

I knew the answer, and I was thinking fast before she got to me. Betray myself as the nerd I was or feign ignorance to try to be one with the rest of the class? I decided to be one with the rest of the class.

"Jean?" Mrs. Pettigrew had an expectant look on her face.

"I don't know," I said, feeling as though I'd let the teacher down and exploded her faith in me. Not that it gained me much traction with the in crowd.

One of the in crowd was Thomas Tarkington Wellman III, Tark for short. He was my red-haired, freckle-faced obsession. Tark didn't have a clue that I was about to expire for love of him—or that I was concocting elaborate fantasies about how he would suddenly be shaken from his indifference with the stunning realization that he was madly in love with me, despite the fact that he had never spoken to me. I imagined that he would pluck me, like a hidden diamond, from my quiet obscurity.

That was before our field trip to the art museum in Richmond. I arrived early, one of the first to board the diesel-smelly Greyhound bus that was waiting for us in the school's parking lot, its motor humming from beneath its big silver belly. It was my habit to always have a book with me, somewhat like the security blanket I dragged around as a toddler. But this time, I'd forgotten my book, and I felt naked and panicky as I picked my way between the bus's shabby velvet seats. My eye fell on an Archie comic book, shimmering on the cushion of an empty seat. What I would have disdained at any other time looked like salvation. I snatched up the comic and settled in the seat with Archie unfurled in front of my face.

Then my heart turned a cartwheel. Tark was boarding the bus. From my vantage point behind the comic book, I watched his every move. He was gawky and coltish, with big feet encased in highly polished brown Bass Weejun penny loafers. His madras shirt was open at the neck, exposing a sugaring of freckles, and he was coming my way! My hands went clammy. As Tark sidled into the seat behind me, I felt faint at the nearness of his familiar thatch of red hair. My own hair prickled when he leaned forward, breath on my ear, and whispered: "I see you've lowered yourself to reading comic books."

I couldn't think of a snappy reply. My head kept saying, "He's making fun of you." So I was silent, interpreting his remark as rejection. For days, I was inconsolable. The next year he went off to boarding school, and I never saw him again. It didn't occur to me that he might have been flirting with me.

# 17

Mom wanted a mink stole for Christmas. The only opportunity women had to show their finery was in church, and furs were the rage at ours. Mom needed to keep pace.

Instead of paying attention, Dad got creative—never a good idea where Mom was concerned—and bought her an antique oak desk that had been designed for a woman. Mom's response was almost a week of silent dinners.

My parents never yelled at each other or fought openly. The only time I knew something was afoot was when Mom gave Dad the silent treatment. Mom never said what she was mad about, but we could usually guess, though Dad was sometimes clueless.

I felt sorry for Dad whenever Mom stopped talking to him. He had shopped for something he thought was special, but he could have made it easier on himself and just gotten Mom what she wanted. With his selective listening, perhaps he didn't pick up on the big hint. The silent treatment worked its magic, and the mink stole appeared shortly after Christmas.

Mom was fond of emphasizing that it was important for her to look good as the "wife of a professional man." Clothes were her ticket to respectability and to allaying her insecurities about her upbringing. I doubt she had much clothing growing up on a farm. What she wore must have been plain and utilitarian. I understood and sympathized with her desire to look good. It was the same for me.

She always dressed up to go out on errands or anywhere in town—a two-piece suit or a dress, stockings,
low-heeled shoes, and the omnipresent jewelry. Her
large collection of Coro rhinestone jewelry—pins, ear-
rings and a bracelet or two—dazzled me. She usually
wore a pin on her lapel. In grammar school, I wore tiny
multi-colored plastic clothespins attached to the pocket
of my white blouse and, later, the popular circle pin.

By this time, Mom was plump. I'd seen pictures of her
when she was younger. In one, she's striding confidently
along a sidewalk, slim in a dark dress that revealed those
good-looking legs that Dad said had attracted him. After
each child, she complained that she couldn't get rid of
the "baby weight." She tried diets but could never stick
to them.

My most vivid memories are of her relaxing in her
brown Barcalounger with Fuzzy nestled on her ample
chest, asking me to fetch her a glass of sweet iced tea, find
the scissors, or grab that catalog she left on the kitchen
table. I always did as she asked, but over time, my resentment began to build. Why did I have to be her gofer all
the time? Why couldn't she just get up and do it herself?
Fuzzy became more her cat than mine, because I never
sat still long enough for Fuzz to spend time on my lap.

Just as I picked up a love of clothing and jewelry from
Mom, I also learned that the silent treatment was an
effective way to express anger or dissatisfaction, and it
took me a long time to unlearn that lesson.

※※※※※

If Mom used the silent treatment on Dad, she had other
arrows in her quiver for me. When I misbehaved or dis-
pleased her, the refrain was, "How would you feel if God
took your mother away?"

"Please, God, don't take my mother," I whispered over and over in bed, as if the repetitions would convince the Almighty that I was truly contrite. I prayed frequently and fervently for my mother's wellbeing, coming to believe that it was my intercession that kept her going. I made a habit of getting down on my knees, propping my arms on the edge of the bed, and folding my hands to reel off a list of loved ones needing protection, but it was always my mother who took center stage. I carried this burden for years, because for years, Mom would finish her Christmas shopping in July. She claimed that she got it done early in case she wasn't around at the holiday. I was terrified into thinking that she could expire at any time and not make it to Christmas. She died at eighty-four.

༄༅༃༄༅

My mother had a thing about not saying yes. Maybe it seemed too permissive in her fundamentalist eyes to say yes, when an "I don't care" would suffice.

"Hey, Mom, can I go over to Sylvia's house?"

"I don't care."

"Okay, great."

But it wasn't great. She was telling me she didn't care whether I went to Sylvia's or not. My takeaway was that she didn't care about me. This was compounded by her other stock response, "Suit yourself." I felt lonely when she said this. If I asked whether I could do this or that thing, "suit yourself" felt less about the freedom to make a decision and more like a rejection. I doubt she meant it that way, but that's how I interpreted it. These responses were her distancing mechanisms; she used them in the same way Dad used humor and teasing to keep us from getting too close.

I have more trouble dredging up memories of her than of Dad, because Dad, especially in the early years, spent time playing with me—from checkers to swimming and fishing at the beach to sledding in winter. He was there physically in a way my mother was not. Neither was emotionally open and demonstrative. They were products of their own love-starved childhoods.

## 18

My mother and her twin sister, my aunt Martha, were much alike in their inability to be close to other people, as was Grandma C. My mother and aunt had a bond through their shared background of deprivation—from the orphanage to their stepfather's farm—and their shared faith. But the affinity stopped at the gate between their respective social statuses. Aunt Martha was jealous of my mother having married up, living in a beautiful home, and enjoying household help. My aunt had not married an ambitious or educated man. Uncle Walter, as an Addressograph (address printing machine) repairman, couldn't earn enough to support the family without her working the night shift as a nurse. Even at a young age, I could tell that she was more envious of, rather than happy for, my mother's situation. She was not unpleasant to me, but I never felt drawn to her, especially in light of the way Uncle Walter and my cousins frightened me and made me feel unsafe.

❧❧❧❧❧

My only first cousins, David and Joe, were part of my life as I was growing up, though I was never eager to see them. David was four years older than I, and Joe was a few years younger. They were plump boys who grew into obese pre-teens and teens, coddled and catered to by their mother, the exact opposite of the treatment I received from mine.

Early visits to the Corsbies, when I was still in grammar school, coincided with Dad's obsession with his movie camera. When we were together, he was always filming the action—behind the camera rather than taking part in the scene. He took movies of us at home, on holidays, playing outside, and on vacations. There were no movies of us with him.

The Corsbie family lived in a modest brick ranch house in Kernersville, just outside Winston-Salem, where my father had wanted to practice dentistry, but couldn't, because he'd been discriminated against for being a Jew. Instead of living near them, as my mother had wished, we visited often on weekends. I dreaded those visits.

As soon as I walked into the tiny living room of the house, with its one sofa and three chairs—a wingback, a barrel back, and one nondescript—skinny little Uncle Walter was on me.

"Jean," he wheedled from the wingback chair in the corner. "Come sit in my lap." I dutifully did as I was asked, but an icky feeling crept in. He kept it up for several years, until I was at least thirteen.

"Tell me. Who's your new boyfriend?"

"I don't have one Uncle Walter."

"Oh, sure you do, pretty girl like you."

His arms were around my waist. I squirmed. All I could think of was, Get me out of here. My parents didn't notice my discomfort. I sat in his lap, immobilized, until I could make an excuse for my escape, usually to go to the bathroom.

Aunt Martha's kitchen was small and dark, paneled in knotty pine. There was a half wall made of pine with a wide ledge separating the kitchen from the dining area and den. My cousins carried around large mason jars filled with sugary iced tea and were never far from the trough—the trough being the ledge of that kitchen divider, always laden with snacks, candy, and leftover desserts. The cousins had rotten teeth, because they were too afraid to let my father work on them, although he would have done it for free. They talked tough, but they were a couple of babies about pain.

David had a collection of Civil War memorabilia in his room, including a saber that belonged to an ancestor who fought for the South. His walls sported a mounted deer head and a jackalope mount—a rabbit with antlers—that someone made for him.

Joe's room featured Nazi paraphernalia as well as a Samurai sword, a Civil War sword, and German daggers—most of them fixed to the cheap paneled walls. A large flag with a swastika hung on the wall above Joe's bed, to the right of the door. I wondered what Dad thought of this. He fought the Nazis. If he noticed, he never said anything.

In summer, we'd play badminton on their front lawn, and they taught me a song to the tune of Reveille that went like this: *There's a soldier in the grass, with a bullet up his ass; get it out Boy Scout, get it out, get it out.* They also used the "n" word. Playing badminton with a racquet in my hand was the only time I felt safe with David.

The two of them, their behavior, and their rooms disgusted me and made me mad. Because they were my only first cousins as well as the sons of my mother's twin sister, I knew better than to act on my anger and disgust. Instead, I tried to keep away from them. Even this strategy failed because my mother encouraged me to "play" with them.

David was always trying to get me alone in his room on some pretext of showing me his latest Civil War acquisition. I was terrified of him, so I dodged these invitations

with a plea to go outside. Joe didn't seem like such a
threat, but I hated his room and the swastika and weap-
ons on his walls.

After one visit, when we got back home, I heard
snatches of conversation between my parents about
David being found in a closet with my sister. I didn't
hear who discovered this or whether my sister told my
parents. They didn't talk to me about it. They carried on
as if nothing happened and never mentioned it again.
Instead of warning us girls to stay away from David, my
mother encouraged me to go to the movies with him.

By this time, he was driving and wanted to take me
to a movie to "show me off." I was nearing fourteen and
had never been to the movies with a boy. Revulsion does
not begin to describe my feelings about this adventure.
David weighed three-hundred-plus pounds, had terrible
acne and bad teeth, and was the last person on earth I'd
want to be seen with.

"No, I can't go, David," I said.

"Sure you can," David said. "I'll even buy popcorn."

As I began to protest further, my mother intervened:
"Now, go on and go with David. You can be nice to him;
he's your cousin."

Despite my air of desperation, my mother would not
tolerate a "no." She would shame me until I relented.
So, I relented.

David opened the door to his rusted old Ford, and
I got in, hugging the passenger door and gripping the
door handle just in case. He hefted himself into the driver's side. The car groaned under his weight, his belly
pressing into the steering wheel. We drove in silence; I
was in no mood to make chitchat.

Once we arrived at the theater and parked, David
tried to take my arm as we walked to the lobby. I pulled
away. Mom wasn't there to tell me to be nice. I tried to

put as much distance as possible between us, pretending
I wasn't with him. As soon as we were inside, he got in
line at the concession stand and bought a huge tub of
popcorn, a Milky Way, and a Dr. Pepper. He asked me
if I wanted anything. I said a quick, hushed "no," and
went to the restroom. I felt as though I would throw up
from the stress of keeping away from him. I stayed in
the bathroom until it was time for the movie to begin.
When I came out, David was waiting for me in the lobby,
one arm around the tub of popcorn and the other hand
holding his soda and candy bar. My stomach took a dive.
I marched ahead of him into the theater and stood by
the wall as though I were eyeing the best seats. David
found two, but it was only when the theater went dark
that I slipped into the row to sit by him. Luck was with
me, and there were three free seats, so I left an empty seat between us. David tried to move over, but I rose
from my seat as if to leave, so he gave up.

We left the theater as we had come in—me steely and
determined to stay away from him, he trying to get close.

I made it through the ordeal and bolted from the car
when David pulled up to my aunt's house. My mother
and aunt had the nerve to ask if we had a good time.

"It was a good movie," I said. There was no way I could
tell my parents or my aunt and uncle how afraid I was.

For years, I was stony and reserved around my mother's other male relatives—her half-brothers and cousins—until I could determine if they were safe. We didn't
see them often. Yet when we did, I shrank from any physical contact—even a harmless hug. Since my mother
had six half brothers and sisters, in addition to her twin,
there were plenty of uncles to be wary of.

❧❧❧❧❧

In contrast to my first cousins on my mother's side, I had second cousins on my father's side whom I was eager to meet. Some of them lived in the Bronx, and a few of the elders spoke only Yiddish. The girls my age took dance or music lessons. I was envious. Since Dad was an only child, I had no first cousins among the Kossoffs.

When I was sixteen in the summer of 1964, my parents put me on the train to New York and a week with Grandpa Herman and Grandma Sadye. I was excited about taking this adventure on my own. My grandparents greeted me with the diminutive I loved, Jeannie. No one else called me that, and it made me feel special.

They lived in Mount Vernon, in a two-story stucco house with a postage-stamp front lawn. They occupied the top floor while renting out the first floor. Two majestic Steinway grand pianos, one a baby grand and the other a parlor grand, stood in a glassed-in parlor off the living room. A bust of Beethoven scowled at me from atop the parlor grand. This was where Grandpa Herman taught piano.

Those two Steinways represented all the art, music, and culture I felt deprived of at home. I experienced such things only at a distance through Grandpa Herman and the books and music he gave us. Dad had traded in his cultured upbringing, or at least the culture he was exposed to, for more earthy pursuits like hunting and fishing. He had taken up those pastimes as a teenager during his summers at Lake Taghkanic.

I wondered if I could ever measure up to what Grandpa had achieved. I desperately wanted to play the piano like a professional and speak fluent French.

The living room featured Grandma Sadye's green brocaded sofa and armchairs, all encased in plastic covers that stuck to my skin whenever I got up. Their separate bedrooms were sparsely furnished. Another room served as a dining room and library—filled with books on

philosophy, art, history, and music—and the glass-front-
ed mahogany cases that held Grandpa's mountainous
collection of sheet music.

If the front room was Grandpa's domain, Grandma
Sadye ruled the kitchen. Roast chicken was her claim to
culinary fame. She would dress the bird and rub the skin
with sage, garlic, and butter, letting it simmer in its own
juices. The smell of roasting garlic permeated the small
apartment and set my taste buds quivering with anticipation. Along with the roast chicken, there would be ge-
filte fish and matzo ball soup, both of which I accepted
as tasty, if underwhelming.

Since I was used to those church potluck dinners with
a cholesterol content that would sink an aircraft carrier,
I was in taste bud culture shock. Grandma Sadye's green
beans were cooked crisp and tasting of spring rain, unlike the Southern variety I was used to—a gray mushy
pulp flavored with fatback or bacon. Instead of scram-
bled eggs, bacon, and biscuits for breakfast, there would
be lox and bagels. The bagels I could devour. The lox I
wasn't so sure about.

For lunches, Grandma Sadye served kosher pickles,
salami, and corned beef on rye or coarse black bread.
These lavish spreads were her welcoming mat. One long
meal rolled into the next, so that eating and talking
filled the hours of my visit.

Grandma had a hard time getting a word in when
Grandpa was holding forth. He eclipsed her and there
was no way she could compete, though I didn't doubt
that she was equally articulate. I understood that she
played the supporting role in the story of their marriage.
But I knew she had managed to carve out a life for herself, outside Grandpa's shadow, with her philanthropic
work for UNICEF.

Grandma Sadye and I could talk when she took me

to her dressmaker to look at clothes—a sharp contrast to the Belk's basement where I shopped with my mother on a tight budget.

"Grandma," I asked, "is this where you always buy your clothes? I've never been to a dressmaker's shop like this."

The shop was small and intimate with velvet-covered chairs and a model who appeared from behind a curtain several times, wearing different outfits for my grandmother to appraise. I felt like royalty once removed.

"I've been coming here for years, Jeannie," she told me. "They know what I like and how to fit me. I thought you should see it." I didn't get a dress out of the visit, but I loved going there anyway.

After visiting the shop, we boarded a train to meet my Bronx cousins. "They're good students," she said, "well-read and talented." She knew I was well-read, too. Did she speak of me that way, I wondered.

I knew of them only through Grandma Sadye and had never met them before.

As we neared the stop for the apartment where several cousins, three girls and a boy, had gathered to meet me, I was anxious about whether they would accept me—a shy, introverted Southern girl with no performing talents to show off. Feelings of not being good enough raised their ugly heads. Instead of being judgmental, they were warm and welcoming. As Grandma had promised, they were budding musicians and ballet students.

I watched with awe and envy as one of my female cousins showed me some ballet turns followed by another who played a Chopin waltz on an upright piano in the parlor. Though I could play the piano, I was too shy and far below my cousin's level to do so. Why couldn't I be closer to *these* cousins? I felt a kinship with them. We had similar interests that I didn't share with anyone back home.

I would gladly replace my first cousins David and Joe and their antipathy toward Yankees with my sophisticated and lovely Yankee second and third cousins. My North Carolina cousins I thought of as rednecks that I would never voluntarily choose to be around. Yet I was forced to see them at least monthly, whereas my exposure to my more distant New York cousins came only that one time. Still, I identified more with my "Jeannie" side and my Yankee Jewish roots. I looked more like them, and we had similar tastes. I wanted to be like them. My war-obsessed first cousins were just embarrassing.

## 19

Many members of the New York side of my family had good business sense. One branch of the family tree included wealthy owners of a mattress firm and lived in a huge apartment on Fifth Avenue. Dad was likewise prescient when it came to investments and buying land, though sometimes we doubted him. His mind was always churning, looking for opportunities that others might not see. In the '60s, flush with income from his dental practice, Dad went on a buying spree. He had already acquired 125 acres in Pittsylvania County just outside Danville—the land he wanted in order to raise cattle. He had his own office building constructed on land he bought across from Danville Memorial Hospital. He rented out half of it to another professional. A couple of years later, he purchased four lots at Smith Mountain Lake, a man-made reservoir that engineers created by damming up a branch of Rich Creek.

Dad described the cottage he would build along with a dock for our motorboat. "It'll be a one-level frame house with a wood stove and electric baseboard heat," he said. "Plus it will be pine-paneled." Dad had a thing about paneling long after it had gone out of fashion. No one could ever accuse him of being trendy.

We'd learn to water ski, he promised. He and Mom could fish. Mom was not unhappy about this investment, but it would mean another, though much smaller, house to care for.

"Let's take a trip to Smith Mountain and see the lot," Dad said one Saturday morning, so we all piled into the station wagon to visit Dad's latest acquisition.

About sixty-four miles from Danville, our part of the lake was accessible by a number of back county roads, one of which took us by Otey's odiferous hog farm, as we later dubbed it, an olfactory road marker that alerted us we were getting closer to the lake. Once there, we pulled into our future lakeside home place, a clearing surrounded by pine and hardwood trees

We looked onto a huge mud hole punctuated with stumps, felled tree limbs, and clumps of twigs, with a puddle way out in the middle, no bigger than a swimming pool. Some miles away lay the blue-green outline of Smith Mountain, directly across from our land.

"You've got to be kidding," I said. "This is just a mud puddle."

"By this time next year, that puddle of water will reach all the way to the edge of those trees over there," Dad said, pointing to a small jungle of underbrush and a few scraggly pines on the sloping lot. I didn't believe him.

"You have to be patient," Dad said.

Patience was not one of my virtues, something I realized early on.

"With the dam already built, water will fill this reservoir as far as the eye can see."

"Well, all I see is a mess of tree limbs and a big puddle," I retorted.

But the joke was on me, because by the next summer, when our cottage was finished, the lake had indeed risen to our property line, where a boathouse sat. After we moved in furniture, bedding, and kitchen stuff, Dad reduced his workweek to four days in summers, so that he could take long weekends with us at the lake. Not that I necessarily wanted to be at the lake with the family every weekend. I quickly became a first-rate water skier, but there was no fun in showing off to family. I wanted to impress my friends.

Though I wasn't above begging, I was never allowed to invite a friend for a weekend at the lake. Then I bargained for staying home on my own—after all I was sixteen by then—which always was met with a resounding no. Mom rarely allowed me to invite friends home for an overnight when I was in high school. Most of the sleepovers I remember were at other girls' houses. Some of the invitations from friends were last minute, which is the way teenagers—always more impulsive—operate. My mother, though, framed them as rejection.

"If they really wanted you to come, they'd have asked you sooner," was her refrain. My interpretation was, They don't think much of you. You're not good enough to be asked earlier.

I see now that she worked out her insecurities through me. They were sometimes an excuse to not allow me to go out with my friends. I resented this but also bought into it. Her insecurities became mine.

My mother also conveyed to me the importance of clothes for fitting in, for indicating my station in life. Since my mother shopped the Belk's basement and did not support high school fashion fads, I got a job after school and on weekends with Rippe's Clothing on Main Street as a shop girl. I earned my own clothing money so that I could kit myself out with what I knew was fashionable—Capezio and Bass Weejun shoes, Evan Picone, and my McMullen dress and blouse with the Peter Pan collar. Clothes were my ticket to acceptance, or so I thought.

## 20

I attended segregated schools through high school, so I didn't know any black kids. I only knew my beloved Cora and Dickie, a strong young guy who helped Dad with outdoor jobs at home and on the farm. Dad loved Dickie. I loved Cora.

Since Cora's family were tobacco sharecroppers, she would take vacation for a couple of weeks in late summer to help her family harvest the tobacco fields. I so wanted to be with Cora that I offered to help her with handing the tobacco before my school started. I was sixteen at the time. My parents agreed, likely thinking it would be a good learning experience for me.

Harvesting tobacco began by picking the lowest yellow leaves and working your way up, over several weeks, to the topmost leaves, which yellowed last. The next step was handing the tobacco from one person to the next until enough leaves were gathered to tie a bunch onto a pole with twine for hanging in the curing barns. A hundred or so of these poles hung from the rafters of each barn, so it took a lot of handing to get to that number.

It was a sweltering day in August—flies were buzzing; leaves were crackling in the breeze. The humid air carried the sweet pungent scent of the tobacco. We worked seated side-by-side at long rough-hewn tables near the curing barns, handing the yellow leaves from one person to the next until someone down the line had enough to tie a bunch to the pole.

With the sun blazing down, I felt flushed and dizzy once the handing got going, but I kept at it as long as Cora was doing it. She wore an old sleeveless blouse and a cotton bandana around her head. When the sweat ran rivulets down my forehead and into my eyes, I wished I had a bandana, too.

The group laughed and joked with one another as the work went on. If they thought it was strange to see a young white girl working the line, they didn't show it. After I'd been handing for a couple of hours, I noticed how sticky my hands were getting. "What's this gooey stuff, Cora?" I held up my hands, palms forward.

Her face lit up when she smiled. "That's tar, honey. When you get home, be sure you clean your hands real good."

"Cora, do you like this work?"

She gave me a puzzled look, her mouth pursed.

"I don't think about that. It has to be done so we can get the tobacco to market. That's what my family lives on, so we just do it."

"It's such hard and hot work. I wish you lived with us all the time so you didn't have to do it."

"Well, these are my people—my momma, my daddy, and my sisters and brothers. I already have a family." Cora emphasized the word "have."

I hadn't factored in Cora's parents, because I'd never met them. Of course, she loved them. It was selfish of me to want to take her completely away from the family she grew up with and loved. But that's what I truly wanted. I thought of her as my family, though I was too self-centered to wonder what she thought of us.

After the tobacco was strung up in the curing barns, it was left for one to two months to air dry. Once leached of its chlorophyll and a leathery brown, the tobacco was ready for market. Cora's family gathered the cured tobacco and prepared it for "The World's Best Tobacco Market" in Danville.

❧❧❧❧❧

Cora always made my breakfasts and got me ready for school, and it was no different when I started my freshman year at all-white George Washington High School, GW for short, in 1963. After breakfast and getting Cora's stamp of approval for my outfit, I was ready to board the bus for GW and face the world. Unbeknown to me, that world was changing, and Danville was in the middle of it.

I didn't know anything about it, because Danville's daily newspaper, *The Register & Bee*, didn't cover the town's growing unrest in the push for civil rights. The paper's owner, Stuart Grant, who'd inherited the paper from her father, was well known as a staunch segregationist. According to my mother, Stuart was "a piece of work," who swore like a sailor and never bothered with Southern niceties.

In my late thirties, I discovered the town's suppression of civil rights when a colleague at Duke University, where I was working at the time, asked my help in accessing the town's photo archives for the period from 1962 through 1966. He was looking for a photograph of a Student Nonviolent Coordinating Committee (SNCC) meeting that reportedly took place in Danville in 1963. We didn't find the SNCC photos, but we found photos of a young Marion Barry—who later served twice as mayor of the District of Columbia—and a disturbing police photo of a black teenager, in a garage, hanging by the neck from a noose constructed from a system of pulleys. You can't grow up in the South and not think of lynchings when you see a black man with a rope around his neck. The photo haunted me.

My colleague and I went to the public library and searched the microfiche files for newspaper articles from 1963 and found nothing of substance. I learned that we were looking in the wrong newspaper; the town's daily paper hadn't covered the Danville Movement. The only reference to any sort of racial unrest I found was a three-paragraph editorial claiming Danville's "coloreds" were content. The only problem was outside agitators who wanted to come in and stir things up.

I couldn't get the photo of the dead teenager out of my head, and I began to wonder what *The Register & Bee* wasn't telling its readers in 1963 when I was a freshman at segregated GW. Where was I when the racial unrest flared?

In retrospect, there was something spooky—and a couple of childhood friends have used the same word to describe the town—about Danville in the 1960s. Like the polluted Dan River that looked so innocent on the surface, Danville had a dark undercurrent, and we sensed it, even if we couldn't put it into words.

I didn't know that in 1960, a dozen black high school students had entered the Danville Memorial Library and asked to be issued library cards. In response, the town leaders shut down the library. It took a federal mandate to force the library to reopen and admit all Danville residents, regardless of race. That was too much for the white leadership, and they ordered all the furniture removed, so blacks could not sit down with whites at the library's tables.*

I had been inside the public library but rarely used it. Unlike some of my friends and schoolmates, I was

---

*See Len Holt, *An Act of Conscience* (Boston: Beacon Press, 1965) and Arthur Kinoy, *Rights on Trial: The Odyssey of a People's Lawyer* (Cambridge, Mass.: Harvard University Press, 1983).

sequestered in a suburban neighborhood and seldom went into town, except to school.

I also didn't know that same year, black students were trying to integrate the lunch counters and used what the movement called "hit and run" tactics: they'd sit at the counter and then leave quickly before the police arrived. Danville's white diners were caught off guard and wanted to keep the lunch counters to themselves. Mom and I occasionally ate at the Woolworth's counter on her shopping day in town, but we didn't see any sit-ins.

The year I entered GW, 1963, Dr. Martin Luther King Jr. visited Danville three times to encourage and shore up the burgeoning Danville Movement. But I didn't know that.

I didn't know that in early summer of 1963, Judge Archibald Aiken, our grumpy Windsor Heights neighbor, issued a temporary injunction preventing the town's blacks from demonstrating further. At the same time, a special grand jury considered indicting the Danville Movement's leaders under Virginia's pre-Civil War "John Brown" statute, which punished "any person conspiring to incite the colored population to insurrection against the white population." Consequently, Danville's white civic leadership indicted three of the movement's leaders.

Nor did I know that Thurmond Echols, a black high school honor student, defied Judge Aiken's orders and led a group of sixty black student demonstrators to city hall. Police surrounded them and arrested Echols. The others fled. Police chased and beat the students and then turned fire hoses on them.

Echols called his mother to get him out of jail. She was arrested when she got to the jailhouse—on the charge of contributing to the delinquency of a minor by failing to keep her son from leading the demonstration. Echols's father got the same treatment when he attempted to bail out his wife and son.

I didn't know that the night of the Echolses' jailing, the pastor of Bibleway Baptist Church and his wife led a march to the city jail and knelt in the alley beside the jail to pray for the Echols family. Police Chief McCain, the husband of my fifth-grade teacher, trapped the church members in the alley by lining up state troopers, city police, fire trucks, even deputized sanitation workers, at both ends.

When the group refused to leave at McCain's demand, McCain arrested the pastor and a white SNCC field secretary and gave the signal to loose the water cannon on the group of sixty-five souls. The force of the water flung demonstrators to the street like debris, washing some under cars, and tearing the clothes off the minister's wife. As the demonstrators fell, police beat them with nightsticks. Others sustained serious head injuries from the force of the water. Two-thirds of the group had to be treated at Winslow Hospital, the town's only black hospital, which was under-staffed.

June 10, 1963, would become known as "Bloody Monday," the most violent of all days in the history of Virginia's civil rights movement. Judge Aiken would be criticized by the US Justice Department for his handling of the trials of those arrested. Danville named a bridge after him.

I didn't know that thirty state troopers, with tear gas and an armed tank, had moved into Danville to maintain order and that police arrested more than two hundred demonstrators.

My life revolved around school, church, and family. Nevertheless, friends who lived literally blocks away from the action told me later that they didn't know anything either. It was a conspiracy of silence by parents, teachers, and the daily newspaper.

Cora, if she knew, didn't say anything to me. Our lives went on as usual.

When Danville was thrust into the national limelight, it was not thrust into my consciousness. Venerable news anchors like Walter Cronkite reported on Danville's resistance to civil rights, but I never saw those broadcasts. I was busy reading or doing homework after dinner.

My parents watched the nightly news. If they watched Cronkite after Bloody Monday, they didn't discuss it. The Southern way was to make nice, not to air dirty laundry or allow any distress to sneak into public conversations or private ones at home. Parents, if they knew about the struggle, must have wanted to protect their children from the knowledge of such "unpleasantness."

Danville had a weekly paper, *The Commercial Appeal*, which did cover the civil rights movement. I knew about the paper only because I saw it in newspaper stands around town. Charles Womack, one of Danville's leading businessmen and a two-term city councilman, was the publisher. His son, David, was my unrequited high school crush. The senior Womack paid a heavy price for speaking out. He lost friends and received threatening phone calls from the Klan. I learned this some twenty years later, when I thought I would write a book about Danville and civil rights, and I interviewed Mr. Womack, then in his eighties.

Looking back, it's ironic that, while Danville's blacks were deep in a struggle for basic human rights, nothing about the civil rights movement was mentioned in my civics class. I was in Latin class reading about the lives of the Roman emperors whose rule was absolute and who understood slavery as the natural order of things. Centuries later, we hadn't come very far.

And our church? Not a whisper about the plight of the black citizens of Danville. I remembered some old saw about "if God wanted the races to mix, he'd have made them all one color." Later on, this made me furious. How did the segregationists know what God wanted?

Twenty years later, I read a book about the Danville Movement. I learned there was only one white minister brave enough to speak out in defense of equal rights—Rev. Robert McCann, minister of First Baptist Church, one of the anchors of Main Street located only a few blocks from our church, West Main Baptist. The church's response was to exile him for being too liberal, so Rev. McCann left the South to lead a church in Boston.

I just finished my freshman year at GW and was getting ready for vacation Bible school at our church, blithely unaware of what Thurmond Echols and other black students my own age were grappling with that summer. I lived as if encased in one of those paperweights with the idyllic scenes inside, the kind you shake to make the snow glitter around the cottage in the woods.

After I learned the truth so many years later, I felt I'd lost my grip on reality. How could this have happened and I not know about it? What else did I not know about Danville? What did I not know about my own family, Dad's Jewishness, and his feelings and reactions? Since learning what really happened in the 1960s, I have carried the guilt of my obliviousness and not having done anything to help. It doesn't matter that I was only a teenager at the time. I should have known.

## ⋘ 21 ⋙

I saw high school as a way station on the road to college and exiting Danville. I studied hard and continued making straight A's. I was also preternaturally well behaved. One puff of a friend's cigarette satisfied that curiosity, and I never tried to smoke again. A splash of wine or a quaff of beer never entered my mouth. I was a model student. I was a practicing Southern Baptist still trying to keep my mother alive by not acting up.

Despite being involved in activities like the Latin club and the school paper, *The Chatterbox,* I felt I was at the periphery of high school social life. I tried out for, but didn't make, the cheerleading squad, which I thought would be my ticket to popularity. I wanted to be like cheerleader Joan Watson, with her smooth blonde flip and her perfect white Chiclets teeth set off by a gummy smile. Boys seemed to mill around Joan wherever she went, like fruit flies around a peach.

"Not good enough," I thought of myself.

Whether I was the instigator of setting myself apart or was simply not of the temperament or social skill to be one of the in-crowd, I don't know. My girlfriends all had boyfriends who took up their time and devoted attention. Not me. The insecurity and shyness that started in sixth grade persisted. Oh, yes, Mike Starns, the handsome, chisel-jawed star of the football team, regularly rode his red motorcycle to my house—for me to tutor him in math and English. My bookishness and good grades would serve me well further along, but I was not proud of them then, nor did I want them to define me.

My experience with boys in high school was one of longing, of unrequited love. If any one of my few crushes had returned my ardor, I wouldn't have known what to do. Dad, as well as most other males I knew, was a mystery, a riddle I couldn't solve. Even in memory, I find it hard to get close to Dad—his expressions, his voice, his words.

At my sixteenth birthday, I was keenly aware of being "sweet sixteen and never been kissed." This disturbed me. I felt I had failed at one of life's milestones. A football player came to my rescue that year. Guy Ward was a gridiron star at least a year behind me in school who eventually received four football scholarships for a free ride at any one of four colleges. I was tutoring him, too. He must have had a crush on me, because, after visiting the house one Friday evening, he kissed me in the driveway before he left. The curse had been broken.

When I told my parents that I finally had my first kiss, Dad said, "I can't imagine you kissing someone else." This struck me as a weird thing for a dad to say. Was he jealous? Did he think he was losing control of me?

## 22

In my teens, trips north for summer vacation replaced our beloved beach cottage at Nags Head. Dad was not interested in where we wanted to go. He was eager to find good trout streams further afield. For two years, he drove us, along with Cora, to Lake Champlain, Vermont. Grandpa Herman and Grandma Sadye stayed in a hotel nearby, so that provided diversion for me. I enjoyed spending time with them.

I loved the outdoors, too, a passion Dad passed along to me. With our cottage at Smith Mountain Lake, Dad paid homage to his youthful summers at Lake Taghkanic and shared the joy of boating and swimming. My brother and I were the water skiers. Mary and Jane tried but could never get up on their skis. Roger and I, not kindly, called them "butt skiers."

Mom rarely left the comforts of home or cottage for hiking, though she did enjoy fishing. She couldn't swim, couldn't ride a bike, so her options were limited. Dad, on the other hand, was always traipsing around the woods hunting, wading a river to fly fish, or simply working outdoors. When I was younger, I also stayed outdoors, biking, looking for crawdads in a stream near our house, or hanging out with neighborhood friends.

The first year we drove north, the trip was livened with a visit to Montreal and Quebec, before we settled at Lake Champlain. I was keen to use my high school French on the Québécois. My excitement fizzled when my high school French was met with quizzical looks by the locals. But I was buoyant with the thrill of exploring a new exotic city. We had actually crossed the border into Canada, my first trip outside the United States. This whetted my appetite for traveling further afield, for getting away from stifling Danville.

Lake Champlain wasn't a bustling place for teens, but we swam in the lake and stayed shore-side for nighttime bonfires in the fire pit on the beach. I remember the moment of bliss when I stumbled upon a clutch of teenagers sitting around the fire after dinner one evening. The sweet smell of wood smoke and the circle of teens around the pit created a cozy and confessional atmosphere, as if we were knit together by the night and the light and trading secrets that only teenagers keep. We talked and joked and sang, pleased to have found each other in this resort for older folks. I was just sinking into the euphoria of being with my own kind when Dad came out to drag me back to the cottage. "It's getting late, and you need to come in," he said, hauling me up by one arm. I was too embarrassed to argue in front of my new friends.

I was furious. It wasn't late. No one else's parents were concerned. I was singled out. It was bad enough that he'd moved us to the suburbs of Danville, so that I had to beg for a ride to get into town to see friends—which rarely happened—but now, when I'd found some new ones, he wasn't going to let me enjoy them. At that moment, I began to realize how controlling Dad could be. Well, I'd show him. I'd give him the silent treatment I learned so well from Mom.

For the rest of the week, I barely spoke to him, then only when directly addressed. I was trying for the equivalent of the mink stole that Mom had acquired using the silent treatment. My strategy didn't work as well as hers.

Dad forbade me to spend evenings on the beach for the remainder of our stay.

After two years going to Lake Champlain, Dad found a place so remote there wasn't a chance in hell I'd find other teens to hang out with. The summer after I turned seventeen, Dad took us on a two-day driving trip to a fishing camp in the back woods of Maine, near the Canadian border. The tiny town of Jackman had hitching posts, a few ponds in the area, and many trout streams.

I groused that there would be nothing for me to do, since I had zero interest in standing thigh deep in cold water waiting for a fish to snap at a fake fly. The rest of the family wasn't hot on the idea, either, but Dad was adamant. He packed our new green Chevy wagon—Dad was a Chevy man—until it groaned under the weight of suitcases and fishing gear.

He had booked us into a rental cottage that was a living museum from the previous century. It had a wood-burning cook stove, rough wood-framed walls, tiny bedrooms, and not much of a living room. The place smelled of old smoke and must. Upon seeing the wood stove, Mom sagged into herself and said, "Hugh, I can't cook on that thing. What were you thinking?"

Faced with a chorus of wails, Dad busied himself with finding a more accommodating cottage, to which we promptly decamped. It was no great shakes, either, but at least it had an electric stove. The only diversion was swimming in one or another of the ponds, abundant with leeches, which promptly attached themselves to our bodies.

## 23

When we weren't vacationing at fishing camps in the summer, I worked as a dental assistant in Dad's office, where I served two summers in a row. I say served because it felt like a sentence. In those days, there were no dental hygienists, at least that I knew of, so Dad did all the teeth cleaning as well as the more skilled work, and he was busy.

Dad had a longtime dental assistant, the loyal Elizabeth Bray, who had helped him for years, as his scheduler and bookkeeper. She seated patients, mixed fillings, sterilized equipment, and handed him dental instruments that he needed while he worked. Elizabeth had a short, back-combed brown hairdo, wore red lipstick, and seemed unflappable. She became a family friend, and Dad often went hunting or fishing with her husband, Jim.

After Elizabeth Bray retired sometime later, Dad had a string of substandard assistants, one of whom was caught drinking mouthwash. Dad couldn't bring himself to fire her, so Mom told her that her services were no longer needed.

At the time I helped out in the office, Elizabeth worked reduced hours and took time off during the summer. What Elizabeth had done, I was supposed to do.

Well, I was no Elizabeth Bray. I was green and had to learn everything on the job. Though Dad paid me, it was a pittance compared to the anguish of being stuck with him all day while my friends were at the swimming pool or summer camps or working jobs that didn't involve their fathers. Instead of learning archery or sailing or canoeing, I was learning to mix amalgam fillings, set out instruments on trays, and then sterilize them before the next use. But who was I fooling? If I hadn't worked for Dad, I would be languishing at home. At least the job got me out of the house.

I ushered patients to the dental chair and clipped the paper bib around their necks, while daydreaming I was somewhere else—Europe maybe. Dad barked orders: "Jean, I need a pair of forceps in room two; Jean, mix an amalgam filling for room one, and hurry up." I still wanted to please him, so I worked hard at getting things just right, just the way he liked them. The smells I remember were the metallic odor from mixing the silver powder with mercury for fillings and the minty scent of the Clorets chewing gum Dad kept in his mouth so as not to offend a patient.

Though I resented working under Dad, I saw his softer side at the office. It was difficult to keep him on schedule because he loved talking with his patients. In return, they adored him. He didn't get upset when some couldn't or wouldn't pay. Sometimes he accepted fresh vegetables or canned goods as payment. Why couldn't he be as generous with me, I wondered. It was as if he treated everyone outside the family much better than those of us close to him.

Once, a patient who had just returned from Florida gave Dad a baby alligator, which he dutifully brought home and installed in an aquarium. Mom was not happy about the new addition to the family, but Dad took good care of the reptile, occasionally putting it in our bathtub to scrub its scaly hide with a toothbrush. He treated it to raw liver and was sometimes bitten for his trouble. We never named it. Despite the coddling, the alligator didn't live more than a few weeks. Mom and I were not broken up about its departure.

As with every wall surface in Dad's life, his waiting room was knotty pine, with brown Naugahyde chairs lined against the walls and green curtains at the windows. At one end, there was a sliding glass window behind which Elizabeth or I sat at a desk when we weren't in the back assisting Dad.

Having Dad as my boss was humiliating for a teenager like me. While he was joking with his patients and singing them his silly lyrics, I was always under his thumb. I don't know why I didn't rebel. But how do you rebel when you've been brought up to believe there's a hell waiting if you disobey your parents, if not in the afterlife, then certainly in this one? My mother's favorite admonishing phrase was, "As long as you're living under my roof, you will not..." The threat of being turned out for disobedience was implicit.

# ❧❧❧❧ 24 ❧❧❧❧

By this time, I had my driver's license. If I thought having a driver's license was my ticket to freedom and seeing my friends in town, I was mistaken. Instead, I had a license to run errands for my mother, taking various trips to drug and grocery stores to pick up things on her lists.

"Jean," she said one Saturday morning, "I need you to go to the Piggly Wiggly to pick up some bread and milk. I don't have enough cash, so take the checkbook and my driver's license so you can write a check."

Behind the wheel of Bullet, I pulled into the Piggly Wiggly parking lot and went in to fetch the requisite items. When my turn at the checkout came, I pulled out Mom's driver's license and the checkbook. For the first time, I noticed her birth date on the license, 1915. Holy cow, I thought. Mom's nine years older than Dad. The shock of this revelation was like finding out I'd been born a bastard. So Dad was only twenty-one when he married my then thirty-year-old mother. What a big secret for them to keep. I wondered if there were other secrets. I knew better than to clue Mom into my discovery.

Mom kept this secret until her death, telling my youngest sister that if we put her date of birth on her tombstone, she would come back to haunt us.

## 25

After I'd been driving for a few months, Dad decided he would teach me to drive a stick shift on our little black Renault, the car Mom said had ruined Dad's driving, because it was a small car that cornered nicely. Dad would whip it around like some Formula One driver.

Dad was calm as my lesson started. "Now, you have to learn to coordinate the clutch and the gas pedal. When you start out, release the clutch pedal smoothly as you press down slowly on the gas."

"Okay, got it."

We began on a flat area of road where I could experiment. We lurched occasionally. Once, I flooded the motor. I looked over at Dad and saw his jaw was clenched. This made me more nervous, but I got with the program, and things were going well until we hit a hill, and the car stalled.

"Just give it more gas, now," Dad yelled, as I struggled, right foot on the gas pedal, left on the clutch. The more irritated he got, the more incompetent I became, until finally he said, "Just floor the damn thing, bitch."

I froze.

He yanked up the emergency brake, and I—without saying a word—opened the door, got out of the driver's seat, and walked around the car so he could take my place at the wheel. If it weren't so far, I would have walked home.

The words stung like the lash of a whip. I couldn't speak for the rising knot of pain and anger in my throat, almost choking me. We were silent on the drive home. When we arrived, I ran from the car into the house. Flopping on my bed, I let myself weep inconsolably. Memories of the day he named me Cruella only fueled the tears.

Eventually, I sought out my mother, who was in the family room sitting in her favorite lounge chair, sipping iced tea, and watching television.

"Mom, Dad called me a bitch," I croaked.

"What did you do?"

"Nothing. I stalled the Renault on a hill and couldn't get it started again."

"He shouldn't have said that," she replied—an economy of words that did little to soothe my aching heart. I wondered if she would say anything to Dad about the hurt I felt. All I know is that I never received an apology. No one mentioned the incident again.

The feeling of being blamed for something I wasn't guilty of was a familiar one. "That expression on your face looks just like Grandpa Herman" came to mind, my mother blaming me for unconsciously exhibiting inherited mannerisms, whether real or imagined by her.

❦❦❦❦❦

That same year, I felt pressure against my windpipe when I lay down, and discovered a lump in my throat. I alerted my parents, but they told me it was nothing but phlegm.

I persisted, so they took me to a doctor, and we learned I had a tumor on my thyroid gland. I wasn't happy about being vindicated. I was terrified. Surgery to remove the tumor was in my near future, and we didn't know if it was malignant.

Dread captured and held me down, but Dad said I was going to be fine.

After checking into my room at Danville Memorial Hospital, where all the rooms were green, the nurse noted that I was having my period and said that I might have to be catheterized to get a clean urine specimen. If I had been frightened before, this new threat unhinged me—so much so that the nurse relented and allowed me to try and get a clean urine sample on my own, which I managed to do.

Directly after the surgery and still groggy from the anesthesia, my throat swathed in bandages, I called for Dad. Even though my mother was keeping watch by my bedside in the recovery room, it was Dad's breezy optimism I craved, like the way he treated his patients. He might serenade me with one of his crazy lyrics ("I Dream of Jeannie With the Light Green Skin" was one of his favorites for me) or make some joke about my new selection in neckwear. I could see my mother was hurt that I wanted Dad when she was right there with me, but I knew he would jolly me out of being scared. He didn't come that day, but stopped by later after work, since the hospital was close to his office. Despite his sometimes cruel treatment of me, the visit cheered me and made me feel safe, as if nothing bad could happen as long as Dad was around.

I came out of the surgery with at least half my thyroid intact, and the tumor was benign. So Dad was right. I was fine.

Unlike Dad's calm in a crisis, my mother was easily overwhelmed and could fall apart in an emergency. When my five-year-old brother nearly drowned at Nags Head by stepping off a shallow shelf of sand into the depths of the ferry channel, my mother saw it happening, screamed, and stayed rooted to the spot. In fairness, she couldn't swim, so she must have felt helpless at that moment. A man picnicking nearby saw my brother's head disappear under the water and ran to haul him out just as he surfaced for the third time. Dad was down the beach fishing from the pier and didn't find out what happened until later. When he appeared and heard the story, he said, "Well, son, you turned out to be the biggest fish hauled in today." His making light of the situation was reassuring, like a talisman that could ward off any serious threat to our family's safety.

# 26

Dad had the energy and drive of someone manic. When he wasn't working at his dental practice, he was presiding over meetings of the Roman Eagle Masonic lodge, the Sertoma Club, or the church deacons—or he was at the farm, planning how to section off and use the land. Sometime during that spending spree, he acquired a single-engine Cessna and renewed his pilot's license at fifty, so he could fly himself to the Outer Banks for fishing weekends. Since my mother was too afraid to fly with him, his weekend fishing trips were bachelor events.

Back at the farm, Sandy Creek snaked its way through Dad's property, and at one point, the creek widened to form a swimming hole with a sandy beach. On hot summer weekends, when even the flies were lethargic, Dad would take us for a dip at the swimming hole. The water was cool and refreshing against our sticky bodies. This was the farm's only redeeming feature that I could see. Otherwise, there were acres of pine and hardwood trees, a few overgrown pastures, and what had once been tobacco fields.

Dad proceeded to populate one of the pastures with a herd of Charolais and rented the old tobacco fields to a local farmer, who kept an eye on the cows. Buying beef cattle was a practical move, Dad explained. "Whenever we need beef, we'll slaughter one of the cows and fill up the freezer."

"Ick," I replied. "How can you do that to one of your own cows? It's so cruel. My dad, the cattle baron," I added. Nevertheless, I often went with him to feed the cows or check the fencing. We took Bullet, good for hauling a couple of bales of hay.

Dad would pull Bullet through the gate and right into the pasture, a ritual I enjoyed, because it seemed to befuddle the cows. There was one breeding bull, however, that was not amused by the appearance of Bullet. Maybe he saw the station wagon as competition. Whatever the reason, this bull decided to charge the car as I was standing by the driver-side door. I knew the signs: he shook and lowered his head and raked one hoof over the grass. Just as he broke into a run, I jumped inside the car and slammed the door. Then, inexplicably, he pulled up short of the door and sauntered away, as if he'd already forgotten the whole thing. Dad had been further down the pasture checking on a pregnant heifer. I told him about my run-in with the bull when he came back, and he guffawed, saying he wished he'd seen that.

The beginning of Dad's troubles came one Saturday at the farm when he was digging postholes for more fencing. It was hard, intense labor, and Dad was middle-aged. The effort earned him a herniated disk for which he would eventually have three operations. The first surgery didn't rid him of back pain, as he'd hoped. His occupation as a dentist, continually hunched over the open mouths of his patients, only exacerbated the problem. But Dad was not someone to take things lying down. He kept up as active a life as he was able, and he continued making plans for the farm. It was his obsession.

## 27

By the time I was seventeen, Dad was fully into planning his dream home at the farm. My sister Mary and I could finish high school at GW in town, but Jane and Roger would have to transfer to rural schools. Living on the farm was a contentious issue in the family. It was one thing to visit the country, splash around in the creek, or come eye to eye with a creamy white cow. It was quite another to be dragged permanently to the far side of civilization as we knew it. My mother, who'd had her fill of farm life growing up, was less than thrilled with the idea of living in the middle of nowhere in Pittsylvania County, the nearest neighbor almost a mile away.

Dinners turned into tension-filled silences, animated only by the clatter of forks against plates or the slurps of iced tea from drinking glasses. I had never seen or heard my parents fight openly. Much of their anger was bottled up. My mother's resistance was soundless. It seemed as though Dad had flung a stone into a still lake, the circles ever widening, and he had taken us from the innermost circle to the outermost, one house at a time. We had a tacit understanding that feelings and concerns were to be kept to oneself, and I had learned over the years that to speak up made no difference.

Regardless of earlier grumbling and silent resistance, Dad was determined that we were going to move from our comfortable rancher, in a neighborhood with kids we knew, to a house he would design. The farm, the house, and the barns would be his monument to a life he couldn't have imagined as a boy, when he took the train into Manhattan at twelve years old and wandered the streets.

The house grew into a two-story brick colonial with walnut paneling throughout. The paneling prompted another debate. "It's going to make the house awfully dark inside, Hugh," said my mother.

"Yeah, Dad," I chimed in. "We want to paint our bedrooms and pick out the colors."

"What difference will it make to you?" he said, in a tone I recognized as this is the end of the discussion. "After all, you'll be in college, and you won't be living here that much anyway."

As in everything to do with the farm, Dad prevailed on the paneling issue. My mother dutifully, though not cheerfully, accepted the dark walnut walls. Since Dad didn't give a fig for interior décor, Mom could do what she wanted with the rest of the house. That was women's work, and I gladly pitched in, because picking out carpeting and the colors for the Formica countertops involved some creativity, instead of slapping expensive wood paneling on every wall.

Dad's dream farm didn't end with a brick colonial house and pastures for his herd of cattle. His vision was grander: there would be a separate indoor pool in its own pool house, a hanger for his Cessna, and a landing strip, so he could take off from home and fly to Nags Head for fishing. He stowed an old car at the Outer Banks airport for transportation once he landed.

He promised that if I didn't put up a stink about moving to the farm, he'd get me a horse. I'd begged for one every Christmas since I was nine, and all I'd gotten were two lousy ceramic horse heads to hang on the wall of my bedroom. I even wrote a fawning fan letter to Arthur

Godfrey, of the famous—at the time—*The Arthur Godfrey Show*, because he raised palomino horses. In return, I got an autographed photo of Arthur on his palomino, Goldie, which I proudly hung on the wall of my bedroom. I only learned much later that Godfrey was a blazing anti-Semite.

I'd read all the horse books from *Black Beauty* to *Misty of Chincoteague*, and I thought surely once the pastures had been readied for the cows, a horse could not be far behind. The horse never materialized, just like Grandpa Herman's promised trip to Europe with me never came to pass.

## 28

As I approached my senior year in high school, the college issue became a thorny one. Dad said, "Jean, I think you should go to Averett College (in Danville), so you can live at home."

Scenes of continued isolation and Dad getting all in my business rose before my eyes. I imagined he would ruin a date, given the opportunity. Fortunately or not, I only had a couple of dates in high school, so he was deprived of the opportunity to be the forbidding father, just as I was deprived of much experience with the male gender. All I had were my fantasies to assuage my flooding hormones.

"No way, Dad."

Dad was peeved I wouldn't go along with the plan he'd obviously worked out some time ago, so he set conditions on my college applications.

"You can go to any school you want," he retorted, as he puffed on his pipe, "as long as it's state supported and in Virginia. And you'll have to help pay for your education by taking out a state teachers' loan."

"But Dad," I said, nearly in tears. "I have no earthly interest in teaching."

"Those are my conditions," he replied, eyebrows knitting together while relighting his pipe and sucking on it with a soft pop. "Take it or leave it."

I took it. My mother tried to soften the blow by arguing, "You'll want to have teaching or nursing to fall back on if something happens to your husband," as if my future was set. All I had to do was walk into it. Find the right man, have babies, and be a homemaker, like my mother.

Well, no thank you, I thought, but did not say.

As the first to leave the nest, I had to blaze the trail out of town. The University of Virginia was not accepting females in 1966, so my only option for what I considered a good school was William & Mary. It was the only college I applied to. I was accepted.

Dad had bought himself plenty of expensive but unnecessary gifts by then, so I was certain that having me take out the state teacher's college loan was payback for my not staying in Danville for college. He who could be so generous with others didn't extend that generosity at home.

❧❧❧❧❧

In 1966, during spring semester of my senior year in high school, Dad ran for city council as an independent. Council elections were supposed to be non-partisan, so Dad resigned his post as chairman of Danville's Republican Party, which had about seventy members. *The Register & Bee* characterized Dad as a "staunch conservative." The article listed his civic activities. Dad was then serving on the Skyline Girl Scout Council; was past master of the Roman Eagle Masonic Lodge; was a charter member of North Main Baptist Church, which we attended until we moved to South Danville and started going to West Main Baptist; served on the Southern Baptist Foreign Mission board; and ran a clinic for Southern Baptist missionaries. The only thing I knew about his platform was that he intended to find out why the proposed Broad Street Bridge had not materialized and make sure that it did. He had campaigned for Goldwater in 1964, even going so far as to have us kids hand out Goldwater leaflets at the state fair that year, an exercise I experienced as humiliating. I had more pressing things to think about than politics, and I had no political opinions of my own.

During Dad's campaign, we learned exactly what some of Danville's citizens thought of him. On one of Mom's shopping days in town, she invited me along. We shopped at Belk and then ducked into Woolworth for a plate lunch special, featuring meat loaf, mashed potatoes, and green beans; or fried chicken and gravy with rice and lima beans.

A middle-aged man sitting on the stool on my mother's right side commenced a conversation with her. The talk turned to politics and the upcoming election. "I'm not sure who I'm going to support," the man said, "but I know one person I'm definitely not voting for—Hugh Kossoff." I watched silently as my mother let the man talk on, her face impassive. "He's a damned Yankee and a Republican, and he doesn't know a thing about this town. If that Jew doctor thinks he knows how to run this place, he's got another think coming."

When the three of us stood up to leave after lunch, the man introduced himself and said, "I don't believe I got your name, ma'am."

My mother, who had been waiting for the moment and whose eyes narrowed and face only then began to redden, replied, "I'm Mrs. Hugh Kossoff, and none of those things you said about my husband is true."

The man's jaw dropped. He cleared his throat, excused himself, and left. In the aftermath, my mother fumed, and I was quiet. I was too hurt to feel angry. This one thoughtless, clueless—and in my memory faceless—man confirmed what I had suspected about my family but never allowed to surface in my mind—that we were different and not acceptable in Danville, that Dad would always be a foreigner in his adopted town, that he would always be considered a Jew. How long do you have to live in the South not to be a "damned Yankee"? More than the fourteen years my father had left to live, that's how long.

I remember my mother relating this story to the family, but I cannot recall Dad's reaction. I can only surmise that he was hurt by such an outright expression of anti-Semitism and took it personally.

Dad lost the election that summer and got fewer overall votes in South Danville precincts than in those of North Danville, according to the daily paper. He was better accepted among the working-class men he liked to hang out with, and they lived in North Danville. They were less concerned about pedigree than South Danville denizens.

My mother wrote me in November of my freshman year in college that Dad was still so upset, he forgot to wish her a happy birthday on her November 9 birthday. He told her he was a born loser.

Given all that he had accomplished, I was stunned that he said such a thing about himself.

I see now that we were marginalized. I had been trying to conform to a standard I didn't fit. Dad didn't fit the standard, either. He had given up his Jewish identity to become a Christian. Still, in the eyes of many in town, his Yankee Jewishness clung to him like a bad odor that no amount of deodorant could cover up.

## 29

When I left for college, I told my parents that I loved them and that I would visit always, but never to expect me to come back to Danville to live. I was homesick for the first few weeks of adjusting to my roommate in Barrett Hall—along with the shock of sharing a bathroom on the floor with other women—and navigating college social life. But I soon settled into a routine of going to classes and writing papers. If I felt free from the constraints of my parents, I still shouldered the burden of anxiety about making good grades and fitting into my new life.

I started out as an English major, on an advanced English track. But freshman composition class cured me of that. My first paper came back with a C, a grade I'd never gotten throughout grammar and high school. This did not sit well with me. I finally worked up to A's in that class, but I had soured on English.

The turbulent times and the Viet Nam war made sociology seem more relevant. Lyndon Johnson was president, and the fight for civil rights was still ongoing, along with the advent of Black Power. The counterculture was beginning to coalesce against the war, and feminism was making its way into the mainstream.

I began to question my religious beliefs and my sense of what it meant to be female in a male-centric culture. I also dropped my Southern accent, as neatly as shedding a coat. Once I was around students from northern

Virginia and the DC suburbs, I could hear my Southern twang and felt embarrassed by it, thinking other students would consider me dumb because of it. I heard myself say "tin" for "ten" and "hah" for "hi," so those were the first two words to change. Since I had a good ear for language and had taken four years of Latin and two years of French in high school, I mastered the art of almost accentless American English in no time.

Because I'd never had so much as a written card from Dad, I was surprised freshman year to receive two letters from him. His first letter came in mid-October, when I was still adjusting to dorm life. In it, he told me not to be discouraged about meeting people whose friendship I didn't want to share. He wrote, "I found the same problems to exist on the campus as well as in the armed forces. I was never happy to associate with people whose moral values were not what I was accustomed to. I never did bring myself down to their level, although I was never fussy about economic status or cultural levels."

I must have mentioned in a letter home that some students I met at W&M were big partiers and drinkers. Southern Baptist teetotaling was still part of my moral framework my freshman year, even as I strayed from my parents' conservative views. At first, I assumed the moral values Dad was referring to were those of the Southern Baptist variety, but then I remembered he wasn't a Southern Baptist when he was in the Army Air Corps, so I wondered exactly what moral scruples he was talking about when he put both military service and college in the same bag.

Dad went on to report that the footings for the new house were soon to be poured and that the roof would be on in less than a month. He segued from the new house to the cottage at Smith Mountain, writing how beautiful the lake and the changing leaves were. He said he sent Rusty, our Irish setter, to "school" to learn to be "a good little bird dog, I hope. I sure do miss him."

He finished the letter by telling me that the city manager resigned and the city engineer "was given the sack on making some money on the Goodyear deal."

I still have that letter with a note, "first letter from Dad," written on the envelope.

His second letter arrived in mid-January of my second semester. He said he approved of my getting into the W&M chorus and not to be worried about grades, that professors "like to keep their classes scared. It gives them a feeling of power."

He missed my "cheery" face at the table. He went on to tell me about going duck hunting, selling our house in Windsor Heights, and progress on the new house at the farm. For some reason, he needed to report that he was paying the portion of my tuition not covered by the state teachers' loan. He wrote about getting furniture for the new house at cost plus 20 percent. The letter ended with a note about Grandma Sadye being back in the hospital for shock treatments. His reaction to Grandma's travails was to say, "I spoke to her on the phone, though, and she was able to carry on a pretty good conversation."

On reading about Grandma Sadye, I felt guilty that I wasn't writing her as regularly as I did before entering college. Surviving in college was all-absorbing.

Dad's mentioning tuition in the letter was a sore point. Given his splurges on big toys like the Cessna and the swimming pool, I knew my tuition couldn't be a financial hardship. Plus, I was paying part of the freight myself with the loan and would graduate with financial debt, because I had no intention of being a teacher. I worked part time at W&M's Earl Gregg Swem Library to earn money for my expenses beyond tuition and meals. I wanted to believe that he was happy to provide me with a good education. Instead he was reminding me that he was paying the bill.

The "estate" house at the farm was completed during my freshman year. I spent time there at holidays or on weekends when I came home to visit, but never felt that it was home. The house in Windsor Heights was the one I identified as home. It was where I loved Cora, transitioned from childhood into a teenager, and had friends to hang out with.

Dad, of course, had been working hard during my freshman year to flesh out his vision for his estate, suited to his needs. About eighteen months after the move, I came home at Thanksgiving to find the pool house complete—so Dad could swim to help his aching back—as well as the landing strip, a wide green swath behind the house and pool complex. Dad's Cessna perched in its own hanger.

Dumping English for sociology was the direct result of my first sociology course with Professor Marion Vanfossen, an impassioned proponent of equality between blacks and whites. I learned about the legacy of slavery and how it still persisted and kept many blacks at the margins of society, which I certainly had seen for myself in Danville with its separate water fountains and bathrooms and its segregated schools. I had seen how Cora couldn't dine in a restaurant with us.

I read Gunnar Myrdal, a Swedish economist and sociologist who would later win the Nobel Prize. His book, *An American Dilemma: The Negro Problem and Modern Democracy*, was influential in the 1954 Supreme Court decision *Brown v. Board of Education*. Myrdal noted what to me was the ultimate hypocrisy of my country—that it still questioned the value of black Americans even after it defeated the Nazis and their racist ideology. Our classroom discussions and my reading fired me up in a way

I'd never known, and I was eager to share my ideas with Dad when I visited during breaks and holidays. His viewpoints differed starkly from my developing liberal ideas.

"Here's my little commie pinko daughter," Dad always said when I came home for breaks. The rest of the family watched our dinner table debates as if they were on the sidelines of a tennis match.

"If that means I'm against the Viet Nam war, then you're right, Dad. We have no material interest in being there, and we're just sending young men of my generation off to die in this endless conflict." I was proud of myself; this was my first chance to show my parents what I was learning and who I was becoming.

"No, we're fighting the commies. The Cold War is still on, and we can't let more countries fall under Soviet influence. If Viet Nam goes, other countries in Southeast Asia will follow, like dominos."

"But Dad, the French failed in Viet Nam. What makes you think the US can succeed? Not to mention that we've been supporting a dictator in South Viet Nam."

"I don't like Lyndon Johnson, but he is right to commit more troops. That's the way we'll end the conflict and the Soviet takeover."

"I totally disagree with you. I don't think this war is winnable, and we're throwing away lives and resources in a fruitless fiasco."

Though he probably thought college had corrupted me, Dad seemed to respect my ability to argue my point of view. Our dinner table disagreements were the only way we connected. Even it if was quarrelsome, it was better than nothing.

The Cold War had been serious business to Dad, who had built a fallout shelter at one of our houses. The shelter was a rectangular underground bunker, big enough for a family of six, lined with lots of shelving that he had stocked with canned goods and gallons of water. There were sleeping bags, but I don't remember his plan for toilets. After seeing inside the place, I quipped that I might rather die in a nuclear attack than spend months of my life in a dark hole. Still, I was glad we had something more substantial than our desks at school. The "duck and cover" drills and diving under our desks seemed less than optimal. Along with our other lessons, we were taught to live in fear of a nuclear Armageddon.

Dad's Republican politics revolved around his worry that the country was "moving toward socialism" and that "the communist party was becoming increasingly active." He pronounced such a warning in 1965 to the Dan River Future Farmers at their awards banquet, where he was featured speaker.

At W&M, I wasn't worried about the communist party. I was more concerned with immediate things, like whether to drink at parties and betray my "alcohol is evil" upbringing or resist temptation and be ostracized. A tall, lanky blond guy I dated once or twice helped me jump that hurdle in my sophomore year. I was smitten with him and didn't want him to think me a square, uptight date. At a party one Saturday night, he urged, "Go ahead and try it. If you don't like it, then you can make a decision. But at least you have to try."

Unable to argue with his logic, I sipped a vodka tonic. Not too bad. The mixed drink signaled the end of my Baptist-imposed prohibition era, and I was more comfortable having an occasional drink, though I never became much of an imbiber.

For the first couple of college years, I was a member of the Baptist Student Union and kept my belief system, no questions asked. Two courses changed that. One semester, I took Old Testament and the second, New Testament. These courses taught me about the origins of the Bible as well as the historical Jesus in the context of his social and political times. I began to view the Christ figure as purely a human being, as Jews did, and wondered if there had been a need for the early Christians to deify him. Those two classes triggered a journey to scrutinize my faith. I read the great theologians Paul Tillich and Martin Buber, the latter a Jewish philosopher and theologian. I learned about Buddhism, Taoism, and Hinduism through an Eastern philosophy course.

Examining my own faith caused me to have questions about Dad's. When he and his crew were trying to get safely back to base in a B-17 riddled with German bullets, he used his promise to convert as a bargaining chip with God. He was afraid and needed a talisman to cope with his fear and believe in his survival. In my view, that was magical thinking.

❖❖❖❖❖

One weekend, my mother planned to visit me in Williamsburg, so I phoned a bed and breakfast that someone had recommended. The proprietor had a vacancy that weekend. I said I would stop by within the hour to put down a deposit. After I walked to the B&B and rang the front bell, a tall graying man came to the door. I told him I was the one who had called and was ready to book the room for my mother. After giving him my name and that of my mother, he said he didn't have any rooms available. But hadn't he told me he had a vacancy and would hold the room until I got there?

When I questioned him about the phone conversation and promise of a room, he got frosty, stated again that he had no vacancy, and then closed the door in my face. I guessed that giving him our family name was the turn-off. It was the only explanation I could come up with to make sense of what had just happened. This man didn't want people with Jewish names in his establishment.

Stung by the rejection and injustice of it, I walked back to my dorm with my eyes leaking tears. This was such a small incident compared to what Dad had been through, yet it hurt me. Dad never showed his pain, but it must have gone deep. Looking back, I wonder if his drive to excel and acquire the trappings of material success was fueled by a need to prove to himself that he was worthy.

When I turned twenty-one during spring semester my junior year, both my parents wrote birthday letters. My mother's was warm and loving: "We are very proud of you sweetheart, and I want you to know, you have been everything we have wanted you to be. You have never given us any worry and any reason not to trust you anytime or anywhere." This was one of the loveliest things my mother ever said to me, and I began to understand that in her way, she did love me, though she could never say it to my face.

I also learned from Mom that Cora was leaving our household for another job. Though I wasn't living at home anymore, I took the news as a personal loss, one that marked my transition into adulthood.

Dad's birthday letter started more formally: "Since your 21st birthday is now a fact of history, I thought it proper to write you a letter on this auspicious time in your life." From that first sentence, he went on to tell me about having a thirty-foot long garage built. "It is covered with galvanized sheet metal and looks very chic. We keep the boat, firewood, junk, and the Jeep in it. Both wagons now stay on the carport." Next he tells me, "I am going to kill another Black Angus heifer on Monday. This little girl is only twenty months old, so it will be some very tender steaks for you to sink a tooth in. The two little bulls are growing like mad."

I didn't want to know about his killing a heifer, especially when he called her a "twenty-month-old little girl." To personalize the animal that way and then have it slaughtered seemed pointless and cruel. But Dad could be cruel at times—consciously or not.

I must have told my parents about a crush I had on a W&M classmate, his facial hair, and the fact that he already had a girlfriend, because Dad wrote, "I was interested to hear about prince charming, but that cruddy moustache ought to go. Just think of all the viruses and bacteria in there when he sneezes. Tough break that he already has a friend."

Ending the letter, Dad wrote: "Well, I must close now, my little mature adult. Be a good girl and don't take life too seriously."

Not taking life too seriously was impossible, not to mention that I had suffered from anxiety and depression since I was in sixth grade, when I faked illness to stay out of school. I had terrible insomnia all four years at W&M. If my parents ever noticed my sadness, they gave no indication, and I didn't know how to talk to them about it. Our family had no language for emotions.

At the end of my senior year in 1970, and after the Kent State massacre in May, I joined a group of students boycotting classes in protest. It was iffy that we'd be allowed to graduate. The school backed down on the threat. I was allowed to graduate, but I spurned my graduation ceremony and got my diploma in the mail. My parents didn't try to talk me into participating in the ceremony. I thought they were relieved not to have to go.

My only real goal upon graduating was to get a job that would take me overseas, as far away from Danville as I could get. The American Red Cross was recruiting on campus, and I applied for a job, because the interviewer told me that I would be given an overseas assignment after one year serving in the United States. I was hired. The Red Cross was my ticket out, and I grabbed it.

## 30

The summer after I graduated from W&M and just before I was to start my Red Cross job, I brought a classmate
home with me. Tall and lanky with close-cropped blond
hair and a blond mustache, Dave Wright had been a
dear college friend after he transferred to W&M during
his junior year. We both worked part-time at the campus
library, found we liked the same books, and wrote poet-
ry. We had long literary and philosophical conversations
and listened to Joan Baez; Crosby, Stills & Nash; Bob
Dylan; The Beatles; and Arlo Guthrie.

Dave was a conscientious objector but didn't get a de-
ferment. Instead, he was assigned to serve as a medic
during the war.

He was fascinated by the old tobacco barns he saw
near our farm and wanted to explore terrain that was
exotic for a boy from suburban Maryland. But Dad had
other plans for Dave. Dad's three hunting dogs—Jake,
Reba, and Dr. Pepper—were housed in a fenced, con-
crete-floored dog lot about two hundred yards behind
the house. With his usual problem-solving approach,
Dad had paved the lot so he could hose it down.

Though I thought of Dave as a friend and not a romantic interest, Dad felt a need to test him. "How about
Dave cleans out the dog lot," he said, more in the manner of an order than a suggestion. Dave gamely took
shovel in hand, with instructions from Dad about hosing
down what he couldn't shovel up, and trudged back to

the dog lot, returning with a sheepish grin and shoes
soled in dog shit.

After the dog lot initiation, I took Dave on a tour of
abandoned tobacco barns and explained to him how the
barns worked, since I knew about it from handing tobacco with Cora. He was intrigued. We stayed for a while at
a larger barn, which was one of the few places we could
be alone without family snooping around. We sat cross-
legged on the dirt floor, hot and sweaty. The sun poked
fingers of light through the slats in the roof.

"I'm sorry about the way Dad treated you," I told
Dave. "He can be embarrassing, and that was no way to
welcome a house guest."

"It wasn't so bad," Dave laughed, "except for having
to clean the dog shit off my shoes."

"Next time we get together, I'll be living on my own.
You won't have to contend with Dad's warped sense of
humor."

Then we were both quiet until I said, "I miss our philosophical debates and the talks we had in our dorm
rooms. I hate that you're going to be sent overseas. I
hate this war."

"I know," he replied. "I just want to get on with my
life without the Viet Nam detour. I even thought about a
future for the two of us together."

"As in marriage?"

"Well, maybe, yes."

This caught me off guard. I had no idea Dave had any
romantic interest in me. I dodged the suggestion and
replied, "That's a sweet thought, but there's nothing we
can do about it now."

I was marriage-averse at this stage of my life. Also, I
was so entrenched in longing for guys who were unavailable that a live, available one scared me. Marrying Dave
never entered my mind, though in hindsight, we might

have made a good match, because we had so much in common.

Dave was the closest male friend I'd ever had, and I was sad to see him leave, sadder still to think of him heading to a conflict zone when every fiber of his being was pacifist.

The day he left, I hugged Dave tight and said, "Write when you can and please be careful out there. I don't know what I would do if something happened to you."

"I promise I'll write and let you know where I'm stationed. We'll see each other when I get back to the states. Please don't worry. I'll be fine." And then he was off to a war we thought crazy and futile, and I wept.

I saw Dave again a couple of years later, returned from the war healthy and sane. He had been assigned as a medic in Okinawa. He told me that he had a serious girlfriend whom he would probably marry. We would keep up a written correspondence for several years until Dave wrote that his wife was uncomfortable with it. After that, I never heard from him again.

## ≈≈≈≈≈ 31 ≈≈≈≈≈

I didn't go off to war, but I did go off to a job that exposed me to the human fallout from that war. My first job with the Red Cross was as a hospital social worker, at DeWitt Army Community Hospital at Fort Belvoir in Fairfax County, Virginia.

Before I left, Dad tried to press a handgun on me. He had gotten a license for it in my name and wanted me to carry it in my purse for protection. He had not discussed it with me beforehand, and I was having none of it. As a teenager, I used Dad's German Luger, under his supervision, to shoot at tin can targets in the backyard, but that was all the experience I ever wanted with a gun. I refused his offer.

≈≈≈≈≈

At DeWitt, I spent my time with a ward full of young men wounded in Viet Nam with lengthy recoveries ahead of them—many made infirm before their time, young men who hadn't chosen to be invalids. Some were suffering from what would come to be known as Post Traumatic Stress Disorder. That syndrome had not been named or acknowledged then.

I rented a studio apartment in a multi-story building, which was all I could afford, and it was bare. I had to repay the state teachers' loan Dad forced me to take out, and my budget was thin as gruel. I discovered I couldn't afford to either rent or buy furniture. I sat on the floor of my empty apartment and wept. Then I had a talk with myself, asking, "What one thing do you need the most?"

That would be a bed, so I bought a foam mattress, which I laid on the bare floor. My parents could have helped, but they didn't. Grandpa Herman came to my rescue: He paid off my student loan. He must have told Dad he was going to do so, but if Dad knew or approved of Grandpa's intervention, he didn't mention it.

Soon after starting the job at DeWitt, I made fast friends with Caroline "Sam" Roberts, a sporty middle-aged single woman with a Prince Valiant haircut and big expressive brown eyes. Sam had spent her entire career in the Red Cross as a recreation specialist. Sam acquired her nickname because she was a pianist and had been in Casablanca during World War II. Humphrey Bogart's line in the movie *Casablanca* was "Play it, Sam."

Caroline/Sam immediately took me under her capacious wing and gave me a green butterfly chair and a small television set for my apartment. She was my friend, my mentor, and the most unique woman I'd ever met. Her family owned much of Block Island, Rhode Island, and Sam had a salty New England accent, a taste for fine designer clothes, and a talent for collecting people who loved her dearly. She was tall and raw-boned but at the same time elegant when she wasn't in the requisite Red Cross uniform, the same one I wore—a blue and white pin-striped dress with a Red Cross pin on the lapel and the insignia patch stitched on one sleeve.

I ate dinner regularly with Sam at her beautifully appointed two-bedroom apartment. Yankee pot roast was often on the menu. She had an upright piano in the living room, along with a large oil portrait of herself as a younger woman in a blue evening gown. She regaled me with hilarious stories. "I tell you, Jean, he was climbin' my riggin'," accompanied by her hearty laugh. We would remain life-long friends until her death from a stroke at ninety.

⧓⧓⧓⧓⧓

I worked with wounded men daily, wounded in both body and spirit. The one patient I remember most vividly was Mr. Butler—a WWI veteran—who refused to have cataract surgery, because he didn't want to be away from his wife. He was going blind, and this would affect his ability to care for her. She was an invalid. Something needed to be done, so I made a home visit, which was a shocker for my sheltered self.

When I rang the bell of their modest frame home, Mr. Butler opened the door, and I was hit with a moist, sour smell, causing me to step back involuntarily, as if I'd been pushed. I steeled myself to follow him into the living room. Everywhere I looked, there were chest-high stacks of yellowed newspapers, probably dating back to when Mr. and Mrs. Butler were first married. I picked my way through the narrow corridors formed by the detritus of a lifetime.

He shuffled ahead of me toward Mrs. Butler's room. I realized then that the newspapers formed corridors that kept Mr. Butler from stumbling into things he could barely see. The late afternoon sun slanting through grimy windows made a halo of his wispy white hair. He was one of those men who, with age, become all bone and sinew, who wear their clothes like scarecrows. Several days worth of white stubble blanketed his sunken cheeks.

"Now, hear me out, Mr. Butler," I said as we moved through the house. "I know you've been waiting on Mrs.

Butler hand and foot for years, but you can't go on unless you have this cataract surgery. You'll soon be blind without it, and where would that leave her?"

"I can manage."

"You don't even have neighbors to help out, Mr. Butler."

"We don't have much use for them," he said. "We keep to ourselves and don't bother nobody. I've been takin' care of things just fine."

I learned that they had no family, either.

When I finally reached the couple's bedroom, I saw Mrs. Butler for the first time. She was propped up in the bed against a hillock of pillows, looking at a magazine. A filthy pink chenille robe covered the mounds of flesh piled up on the sagging mattress. I wondered how and where Mr. Butler slept. It was clear that Mrs. Butler had not left that bed for years. I introduced myself and told both of them, with all the conviction of my callous youth, that I had the solution to the problem.

"I've arranged with the hospital to admit you, Mrs. Butler, at the same time Mr. Butler goes in. That way, you'll be taken care of, and when Mr. Butler is well enough, you can both go home." It had taken me a lot of persuading at the hospital to make this happen, so I wanted no arguments.

"I don't know if I can stand the trip to the hospital," Mrs. Butler said. "I've got a weak heart, and I don't get far from this bed."

"Don't worry, we'll have an ambulance come and get you," I explained. "It's all arranged."

The next day, the hospital admitted the Butlers—the Mrs. to the cardiac ward, Mr. Butler to EENT. I had tried to get them in the same room, but it was against hospital policy. They'd bent the rules enough already, so I didn't press it.

"Are you ready for surgery, Mr. B.?"

"I don't know. I'm worried about the missus. She wasn't well this morning."

"She's doing fine. I just checked on her."

"How soon can we go home?"

"The doctor said, if you're doing well, you and Mrs. B. can go home in a couple of days. The home health nurse will visit for a few days until the bandages come off, then you can go back to your life the way it was."

"I don't like this. I'm uneasy."

"I'll keep check on your wife while you're out of commission, Mr. B. Don't worry. I'll report back to you when you get to the recovery room, okay?"

By the time Mr. Butler reached the recovery room that afternoon, Mrs. Butler was dead—cardiac arrest. I had gone in to check on her and found the curtains drawn around the bed, the residents and nurses rolling the defibrillator out of the room. I stepped behind the green curtains. Mrs. Butler was on her back, head tilted so that her chin pointed to the ceiling. The flesh on her neck sagged.

I had to tell Mr. Butler his wife had died—a task for which my twenty-one-year-old self was not prepared. I waited until he was back in his room, both eyes bandaged.

"Mr. Butler, I'm so sorry, but your wife passed away this morning as you were in surgery. The doctors did all they could to revive her, but her heart was too weak."

There was no flash of anger or outburst of grief. He took the news silently, as if it was what he had expected. I was guilt-stricken. Since there were no family or friends to step in during the crisis, I made the funeral arrangements. I located a nearby funeral home, selected a navy dress for Mrs. Butler to wear, as well as the casket in which she would be buried.

On a cold, blustery November day, we buried Mrs. Butler in Arlington Cemetery in Mr. Butler's veteran's plot. I had gathered a small band of mourners from the hospital staff. They were waiting as I wheeled Mr. Butler to the gravesite, his legs covered by a wool blanket, a bandage still over one eye. As the minister pronounced the final words, a tear escaped from beneath Mr. Butler's bandage and coursed down his corrugated cheek. Dead leaves skittered across the freshly dug earth.

Seeing the Butlers' co-dependence upset me, and I judged it to be a bad thing. I took pride in living alone and being self-sufficient. Mrs. Butler's death humbled me.

## 32

The call came a few days after Mrs. Butler's funeral. Headquarters wanted me in Yokosuka, Japan, right away. The hospital field director there had resigned abruptly, and the Red Cross was short staffed in the Far East. I said, "My bags are packed." At last, an overseas assignment on the other side of the world from Danville. My only regret was, I had developed a crush on a young dentist at the hospital and had finally gotten his attention. That he was a dentist was part of his appeal. If I had left Dad and Danville behind, I was still looking for him elsewhere.

I was booked on a military flight with stopovers in Honolulu, Wake Island, and Guam. A seaman met me at Yokota Air Base and drove me the two and a half hours to the US Navy base in Yokosuka, which is thirty miles southwest of Tokyo, situated on a small peninsula jutting into Tokyo Bay.

On the ride to Yokosuka, I was struck by how miniature the homes and buildings looked, compared to what I was accustomed to in the US. When I arrived, I was both chagrined and amused to learn that I, a Viet Nam war protestor, would be housed in the bachelor officer's quarters—given a spare room with only a single bed, a desk, a chair, and a bathroom.

There I was, six thousand miles from home, at a naval base working in a support role for the US military in a war I loathed. All my dinner table debates with Dad about my opposition to the Viet Nam war had come to this.

I ate in the officer's mess but was left to myself. The officers didn't quite know how to treat me, nor I them, because I thought of them as the opposition. Gradually, I relented and got to know a couple of junior officers who took me on dates off the base. After all, I told myself, many of them were drafted.

One, a sweet but conservative young officer named Reggie, served on the USS *Vernon County*, an LST—a landing ship tank also known humorously as a large slow target. Reggie took me out on a family cruise aboard the ship, when officers, seamen, and their wives and family could come along. A couple of weeks later, Patrick O'Gara, the commanding officer of the *Oriskany* invited my Japanese friend, Satchi, and me for lunch and a tour of the aircraft carrier. I was fascinated by the technology that allowed a navy jet to take off—with the aid of a catapult—and land, using the plane's tail hook to grab the arrestor wires strung across the deck, on such a limited space. The ship itself could hold three thousand men and was outfitted with everything necessary for a long deployment—shops, a hospital, and a dental clinic. Its mission at the time was to launch strike operations in Laos, though I didn't know that then. Missions were kept secret except for those with a need to know.

Since I was almost 5'8" with dark brown hair and light blue eyes, the Japanese in the shops in town always remembered me. If I went into town to buy a specific scented soap, the shop girls would smile, bow, and retrieve the same product I'd bought before. This was a silent transaction, since they spoke no English, and I knew only a smattering of Japanese.

Fortunately for me, the windows of noodle bars and restaurants always displayed plastic replicas of the dishes offered inside. I could point to the pile of plastic, and the servers would know what I wanted. Sometimes, I got surprises using this method—bird's eggs, seaweed, or some unidentifiable but definitely fishy flavor.

One weekend, I had gone into town to shop and was walking back to the base. I was greeted by a demonstration against the likes of me. The residents of Yokosuka always knew when a US nuclear sub was going to pull into port, and they marched in protest. Foreknowledge of this event seemed to make its way from the prostitutes at the pier, who apparently had been with servicemen with loose lips.

On this particular day, I was on a corner waiting to cross the street when a large group of Japanese protesters passed by, shouting "Yankee go home." There I was, the only Yank in sight, and there they were, looking at me and raising their fists. I knew that for every three or four protesters, there was a Japanese policeman to keep order. I wasn't afraid, just embarrassed.

Other than this one experience with the protestors, the Japanese I encountered were unfailingly polite and always willing to help me find my way when I got lost. I was treated with respect, as if I were some rare bird that had landed in their midst.

It took a two-hour bus trip to negotiate the forty miles to Tokyo the first time I went. I learned never to do that again, but to always take the train. I didn't fear traveling alone. I went into the major shops on the Ginza, to teahouses, and explored the back alleys crammed with tiny shops and restaurants. This was a time when Tokyo's air was heavily polluted, and I returned to the base with a thin film of black grime on my face.

Barely past the age of twenty-two, I was the hospital field director for Red Cross operations at the naval hospital, which meant I was to provide social work services for the patients, head up a group of hospital volunteers, supervise secretarial staff, and be on seven-day, twenty-four-hour call every other week.

I was given a small red staff car with a stick shift to drive around base. Since my training in driving a stick had been disrupted by Dad's less-than-admirable qualities as a teacher, I was still not adept with a manual transmission, but I managed to grind-gear my way around the base.

The US Naval Hospital was a rambling, drab, outdated wooden structure. "Oh, for the clean, busy atmosphere of DeWitt," I wrote in my diary. "Everyone here seems to be lethargic," I added. It was hot and humid, and we were working without air conditioning, so lethargy was a reasonable response. Badly wounded soldiers were sent to a more modern facility. That would explain why I saw only a couple of nurses and about as few doctors during my first days of work.

Instead, those wounded in mind and spirit came for treatment. The one exception was Teddy Carter, who was brought in with his guts ripped by shrapnel. He was drifting in and out of consciousness from the morphine and kept calling, "Charlene, Charlene."

One of the nurses told me that the wounded men always moaned the names of their girlfriends or wives; sometimes they asked for their mothers—young men barely out of boyhood calling for the comfort of their mothers' arms. I held Teddy's hand for days until his eighteen-year-old wife Charlene arrived, terrified. Then I held Charlene's hand.

When he was strong enough, Teddy was air-evacuated home, along with Charlene. I never knew what finally happened with him.

The Red Cross management-level duties were challenging. Since the Red Cross provided me no training, I was making it up on the fly. The most hateful part of my job was the twenty-four-hour call I shared with the base field director, which meant that every other week I was confined to base for seven days and was expected to work for seven days if the situation required it. To be cooped up in that hellhole with boredom as my only companion began to make Danville look good by comparison.

From my diary, dated July 1, 1971: "Oh, I hate this job! There are reams of paperwork. The Red Cross runs on paper and getting the most time out of its personnel for the least compensation." I also told my diary that I could not envision myself staying the entire two years, that the base was wretched, and that I felt as though I was in prison when I was on call.

One night, I was awakened at 3 a.m. with a call from communications saying they'd received a wire that a serviceman's mother had died in the US. I got up, got dressed, and with his name and location in hand, drove to his quarters and asked for him. Roused from sleep by the night duty guard, he had pulled on a tee shirt and pants.

"Hi, John," I said. "I'm Jean Kossoff, with the Red Cross." He knew something was up and stared silently.

"I'm so sorry to bring sad news from back home. Your mother has died, and the family wants you to come home right away."

He took a step back, then stammered, "But ha-how do I get there? What do I do?"

"Don't worry about that," I said, trying to smooth his way. "I'll take care of everything. I'm going to ask your commanding officer to grant you emergency leave. Then we'll send a wire back to the US to advise your family that you're coming and get you on a plane home. I'm sorry for your loss," I added, wanting to hug him but knowing it would be improper.

"Thank you," he said, dry-eyed and looking numb.

I made my appointed rounds, ending with the communications station to send a wire to the family and file the omnipresent and oppressive paperwork.

After a night of work and a couple hours of sleep, I rose at the usual time to be at work by 8:30 and put in a full eight-hour day. Those weeks on call were my private hell and passed in a haze of sleep deprivation. On average, I would get two or three middle-of-the-night calls a week, including weekends.

I wrote my parents regularly from Japan and received encouraging and newsy letters from Mom. I don't recall any letters from Dad. This wasn't surprising, since he'd never been much of a letter writer. He'd proven that by not writing Mom the two years he was overseas. She didn't know if he was dead or alive.

Despite the heady brew of living in an exotic country and exploring its wonders, including trips to Mt. Fuji and Kyoto, I began to feel low. If I felt restricted growing up in Danville, I was on virtual lock-down the two weeks a month I was confined to base. The alternate weeks off, I was happier, because I could travel on weekends and had my evenings free to see new friends.

But some nights, I cried myself to sleep, feeling lonely and conflicted. Though I did not miss Danville, I missed my family. On the one hand, I came alive when I could explore Japan, learn its customs, and be among its people. On the other, I felt desperate when I realized a full one-year out of the two of my assignment would be spent tethered to a US naval base, one which some people never ventured from and which I found dull and oppressive. There weren't many wounded vets to help, and there wasn't much I could do for those on the psychiatric ward, except feel awful for them. Since headquarters would not reassign me, the only way to leave the naval base would be to resign from the Red Cross.

Making that decision was difficult because I didn't think of myself as a quitter. When I made a desperate phone call home, my parents encouraged me to return. Though I had wanted to be entirely independent, I had to come to terms with the idea that, at least temporarily, I needed my parents' support. After three months and talking to friends and the Catholic priest on the base about my dilemma, I resigned. The idea that I was running back with my tail between my legs nagged at me, but the relief I felt after resigning was evidence enough that I had done the right thing. I loved Japan and wanted to stay on my terms. I made some feeble attempts to find work that would keep me there, turning up nothing.

## 33

To say that I returned home defeated would be an understatement. Dad had been defeated, too, in his second run for public office—the Pittsylvania County Board of Supervisors. I can only guess at what the second loss, after his unsuccessful bid for a seat on the Danville City Council, did to him psychologically, especially since the first had been such a blow to his self-esteem.

For me, it was back to the farm and Danville until I could find another job, which I was eager to do.

Being home for a few weeks revealed to me just how much Dad had deteriorated, ostensibly from his back problems. He worked a reduced schedule and was often out with back pain. He had a second minor surgery to implant a dorsal column stimulator, a device, sometimes called a "pain pacemaker," that sends electrical signals to select areas of the spinal cord (dorsal column) to treat pain. It didn't work for Dad.

Desperate, Dad prayed hard and constantly for God to heal him. When that didn't have any impact, he reached for treatments like acupuncture and even considered a frontal lobotomy—a procedure that severs the fibers connecting the frontal lobe of the brain. There had been studies in the fifties concluding that lobotomies could relieve intractable pain, but with serious side effects such as personality changes, epilepsy, paralysis, and even death. I was shocked that he was willing to go to such lengths to deal with the pain. While I sympathized with him, I tried to dissuade him from even thinking about the procedure. Eventually, he let it drop.

⊗⊗⊗⊗⊗

While visiting my sister, who was in graduate school at UNC-Chapel Hill at the time, I applied for and was hired as a medical social worker at UNC Memorial Hospital, at the age of twenty-four.

Chapel Hill was fairly close to home—a negative for the young woman willing to go to Japan to escape Danville—but it was a college town with a liberal vibe. I could help out with Dad, who was becoming less and less like his old optimistic, can-do self. He was staying home in bed more than he was working.

Finally, Dad got a diagnosis: multiple myeloma, which causes cancer cells to accumulate in the bone marrow and crowd out healthy cells, back then a dire diagnosis that would account for his back pain. It was also terminal.

I grieved about Dad's condition, but I couldn't let it affect my work at the hospital. I was responsible for patients receiving urology, neurology, and neurosurgery services, as well as serving on the spinal cord rehabilitation team. The work itself could be depressing. Often I would have to help families make arrangements to transfer a loved one who'd had a stroke or brain tumor to a nursing home or, if they were lucky, a rehab facility. I saw young men and women after shattering accidents that left them paraplegics or quadriplegics. I listened to their grief, their anger, and their fear. I was heartbroken for them all.

I was not able to cultivate the professional distance necessary to separate my work from my private life and carry on. I was unable to enjoy the things I usually loved to do after work and on weekends. I carried a pit of dread in my stomach.

Despite the presence of female nurses, the hospital was a man's world, and in that world, the doctors were gods. Many conducted themselves that way. One resident neurosurgeon who would eventually operate on my father—Gerard Pittman—enjoyed harassing me. If I was nearby when Pittman made his rounds with interns and other residents, he liked to bellow out, "Well, hello, Miss Kissoff, how are you," knowing full well what my last name was. He would draw with markers on the foreheads of his patients to illustrate for his male acolytes what parts of the brain he might be targeting. I didn't think much of Dr. Pittman, a tall, dark-haired, lanky guy with a face I've forgotten.

When I'd had enough of being called "Miss Kissoff," I replied to Pittman's usual greeting with, "I'm fine, Dr. Pissman. How are you?" I didn't plan it. The phrase just popped out. He looked shocked, then shrugged. I suppose it got through, because I don't recall Pittman calling me Miss Kissoff again.

Despite my feminist principles, I wasn't above primping in the ladies room in case I ran into a particularly good-looking intern or resident in the stairwell. I dated one or two, but they were generally too tired from pulling long shifts to be much company. One fell asleep at the movies, another sitting on the sofa of my small apartment. I wasn't angry. I felt sorry for them and concerned about what kind of job they could be doing for patients when so tired and overworked. The system was inhumane. At least I worked an eight-to-five job.

Other forms of harassment were commonplace, and most of us women didn't pay much attention: construction workers whistling and making suggestive remarks when we walked by, men on the street looking us up from bottom to top and then letting their eyes rest on our breasts. That, too, began to get under my skin, so

I developed a strategy for dealing with it. Rather than being a passive victim, I would turn and stare and keep staring as I walked, until they were out of view. That shut some of them up. Eventually, I turned to calling them "knuckle dragging Neanderthals," feeling smugly certain they wouldn't know what I was talking about.

My work on the spinal cord rehabilitation team was the most satisfying. One of the first questions the male paraplegics asked was whether they could ever have sex again. Their doctors either ignored or danced around the question, saying it was possible to father a child. But how? They never said.

Recognizing how important it was to my patients to understand their sexual functioning post trauma, I searched for answers and found a conference in Minnesota on "Sexual Counseling of the Disabled." Then I drummed up enough grant money to get myself to it. There were social workers and counselors like me in attendance, as well as what we would now call "differently abled" adults.

The first thing the conference organizers had us do was to shout out sexual terms in an attempt to desensitize us to the material we would be covering. While we were shouting, porn films, including *Deep Throat*, were projected on every wall of the conference room. I had never seen a porn film, but I was neither shocked nor disturbed—nor were they a turn-on. I looked at them with clinical detachment as shouts of "cunt," "dildo," "penis," and "cum" swirled around me. I was not sexually naïve and had given up my virginity at twenty-one, mostly out of sexual attraction and curiosity.

The most affecting part of the conference was to watch films of real disabled people, not actors, making love. Nor were lesbians and homosexuals left out. These films taught me something crucial—something I shouldn't have needed to be taught—that sex is beautiful when it involves two people who are willing to be open and vulnerable to each other and who each cherish and protect that vulnerability in the other, that the best sex is born of love, acceptance, and tenderness. These films moved me deeply. I hadn't known tenderness, nor did I remember either Dad or my mother telling me they loved me. This was a sad realization, but also a hopeful one. Maybe there would be some love and tenderness out there for me.

Back at the hospital, I became the de facto sexual counselor on the rehabilitation team, and my first success was with a male patient, angry and unwilling to talk at first, who finally accepted my help and, after a few months of rehab, married one of the nurses on the ward.

While my contribution to the rehab team was rewarding, I still lived in a world of illness, bad luck, and terminal diagnoses, and I couldn't leave it at the hospital. My world was painted in tones of black and gray. Grieving for my patients and Dad left me drained. In the mornings, I felt glued to the bed, using sheer will power to pry myself off the sheets. Nothing gave me pleasure or joy. I began to withdraw from friends and social life. I saw a psychiatrist, who put me on one of the old tricyclic antidepressants. The side effects made me drowsy and dopey. I came home from work and fell on the sofa, drifting in and out of sleep, unable to do anything else. It felt worse than the depression, so I stopped taking the drug after a few weeks. What good was an antidepressant if it turned me into a zombie?

Being diagnosed as clinically depressed gave me insight into those years of sadness and withdrawal I had had as a pre-teen and teen. I must have been suffering from depression then, too, but unaware that those feelings were not normal.

After assuming and mourning that Dad might not live long, I learned that his doctors reversed themselves and said he didn't have multiple myeloma; it was osteoporosis. How could they have made such a mistake? Were they reaching for a diagnosis that would explain the recalcitrant back pain? We never got any answers.

Dad agreed to a third back surgery to relieve nerve pressure that was causing what the doctors called "foot drop." The nerve impingement left him with a limp because his left foot was dragging a little as he walked. The surgery would correct this, if the nerves were still intact.

When I visited home, only my youngest sister Jane was still living there. I loved Jane and felt sorry that she was left alone to deal with Mom and Dad.

Dad and I still had our dinner table debates, but I was the instigator—anything to get Dad to connect with me. If I didn't provoke him, he was more distant than ever. Those debates were the one thing that brought us together. Even if the talk was fractious, I'd take it.

At the time, I was dating a sweet, handsome black medical student, and I told Dad all about Anthony. It was a defiant move to gauge his reaction.

"Well, don't think you can bring him here," Dad said. "I don't understand what the hell you're doing."

"What if I decide to marry him, Dad?"

"Then you won't set foot across this threshold again."

"I can't believe you, of all people, would say that. How could you?"

He knew the sting of rejection, of being made the other. In WWII, he fought against those who would create a white master race, yet he didn't see the irony. Sometimes I hated him.

⌘⌘⌘⌘⌘ 34 ⌘⌘⌘⌘⌘

My mother phoned me at work in Chapel Hill. "Your father has had some kind of psychotic reaction to the pain medication they gave him after his back surgery," she said. "The nurse told me he broke his water glass and was threatening her with it and then tried to slash his wrists. She went to get help, and when she got back with the orderlies, your father was trying to jump out the window. They had to restrain him."

"Oh my God, Mom. What do you need me to do?"

"You have to leave for Danville right away," she urged. "I've got the flu, and I can't get to the hospital. I need you to find out how he is and take care of things."

During the hour and a half drive from Chapel Hill, I had plenty of time to imagine what I might find when I got to Danville Memorial Hospital—and to dread it.

When I arrived at his hospital room, my father was anchored to his bed, a ghostly white figure, his arms bandaged across his chest as if he were wrapped in a shroud and being prepared for burial. I knew the white binding was a straitjacket, though I'd never seen one before. I knew what a straitjacket meant.

As I walked across the gray institutional tile floor to his bed, my legs went rubbery, and my veins felt full of hot wax.

Dad's eyes swept the room, not taking me in. His crew cut looked moth-eaten, his forehead beaded with sweat. A Styrofoam cup had replaced the glass that had been on the table by his bed. He couldn't get to it even if he wanted to. He couldn't do anything but move his head from side to side.

He was saying something in quick, jerky phrases. At first, I couldn't make it out, because he was panting as if he were running and trying to talk at the same time. Then his words became clear.

"I can't get away from them ... can't run fast enough," he gasped. "They're calling me a dirty Jew. They're going to castrate me. My God, they're going to get me." His arms were working inside the restraints.

"Dad, Dad, it's okay." I said, reaching out to wipe his forehead with a Kleenex I'd grabbed from the box on his bedside table.

He eyed me like some wild animal ready to gnaw off its leg to escape a trap. I groped for words, anything that might interrupt the terrible scene unfolding inside his head.

"Dad, you're dreaming. It's me, Jean. I'm with you now; you're okay. No one is going to hurt you."

But wherever Dad was, I couldn't reach him. He didn't know me. He was still in the street running for his life.

I'd never heard him talk about what it felt like to be a Jew and to have abandoned his ethnic and religious roots or how the war had affected him emotionally. His mind had to be free of its normal restraints for him to let his demons escape. His words shocked me as they erupted from a private well of despair.

In that hospital room with my father, I felt a kind of abandonment I'd never known before. A stranger had invaded my father's body, and I had to reassess my understanding of who my father was. What happened that day would be the beginning of a long process. I had to reconcile the man I thought I knew with the man my father was becoming.

## 35

Once the pain meds cycled out of his system, Dad regained his grip on reality. He got through his psychotic episode and went home to recuperate from the surgery. I phoned my mother weekly and visited when I could to see how my parents were coping. I'm certain Jane's presence at home was a salve to my mother, but I saw the strain on Mom's face. She had to deal with Dad's increasingly irrational and abusive behavior and still try to keep up appearances.

Dad's third back operation relieved the foot drop but not the back pain, which was chronic and robbed him of his cocksure approach to the world. I could see he tried to reclaim the active life he once knew. His former, almost hyperactive, life had been a way for him to outrun his demons. The interlude in the hospital showed how present those demons always were, how close they came when he could not maintain his guard.

I thought of Grandma Sadye's episodes of depression. I saw that Dad was depressed. It didn't occur to me then that he might be bi-polar.

※※※※ 36 ※※※※

During my twenties, I decided to explore Judaism and attended one of the Durham synagogues to see if I could find a home there. The Baptist church held nothing but bad memories for me, yet I wanted to belong somewhere. I hoped it would be with Jews, my father's tribe.

At the first synagogue service I attended, the recitation of Hebrew and the cantor's singing stirred something primal in me. My blood connected me to a long and storied history, laden with both grief and accomplishment, to a people who had set themselves apart and were punished for it—just as Dad had set himself apart from his birth family by becoming a Christian and as I was now setting myself apart from my birth family by rejecting Christianity.

If I thought I would be warmly welcomed at the synagogue and that such a welcome would resolve my feelings of not belonging, I was mistaken. No one approached or greeted me at the few services I attended. It was a closed system. Jews didn't proselytize or look for converts the way Baptists did. Hence, they didn't rush to enfold me and increase their numbers. I felt as much an outsider in synagogue as anywhere else. I realized that organized religion of any variety was not a natural for me. It required too much conformity and too much that was prescribed and proscribed. I would find my solace in the cathedral of the natural world. I would put my faith in science, and I would take my place with the agnostics and atheists.

In all my searching, I was also looking for love.

⊰⊰⊰⊰⊱

Will and I met as singers in the Durham civic choir—
he a tenor and I a soprano. He was different from the
residents and doctors I had been dating in Chapel Hill
during the three years I was working at the hospital. He
was a college-educated craftsman who lived in a Durham
commune—the counter-culture hub of Durham, called
Monkeytop—with roughly a dozen people, male and
female, in an old rundown mansion that had once belonged to a textile mill executive. The group paid twelve
dollars a month each to rent the once stately home and
raised vegetables in a garden out back. Their aim was to
be self-sufficient.

Will's bedroom on the main floor had its own fire-
place, which offered a romantic and cozy opportunity
to fall asleep near a crackling fire when the weather was
cold. We were what I would call conservative hippies. Free
love was okay—but my version involved being committed
to one man at a time, no messing around with multiple
partners. I would have been overwhelmed by Woodstock,
but I was curious about communal living. I thought Will's
lifestyle was exotic—far from my more predictable one
with a regular salary and one-person apartment living.
He was not a "professional man" like Dad, and he answered to no one but himself. Though Will didn't talk
much—no long and nourishing conversations like those
I'd had with Dave—I was drawn by his quiet strength,
self-sufficiency, and his goofy sense of humor.

Will and I rode our bikes all over Durham, though
I had a green Ford Pinto—the car that was recalled
in 1978 for catching fire in collisions—and he had an
old VW bus that he was constantly working on. Neither

of us owned much. He had long hair and so did I. We loved Joni Mitchell and her poetic lyrics—"you are in my blood like holy wine, you taste so bitter and so sweet, oh, I could drink a case of you, and still be on my feet"— and we loved the idea of being hippies, however you defined it. Although the roach clip was passed around often at Monkeytop parties, neither Will nor I partook. I had been dealing with depression and anxiety, and I was afraid of taking anything that might alter my brain, no matter how much fun it promised. I told Will that. I was my father's daughter in many ways.

One of Will's two sisters had committed suicide before I met him. He knew about depression. But he wouldn't talk about his sister. It was off limits for me to even ask. We didn't understand then what a big part depression played in both our families.

One friend said to me that though I looked more con-servative, I was more freewheeling than Will. He had long blond hair, a beard, and wore button-up Levis, but was a fairly conservative guy by nature. He never explored the drugs that were freely available at the time—or sex for its own sake. He had been faithful to his former girlfriend. He had a solid work ethic, even if it didn't involve a reg-ular job or working for someone else.

When I was not at work, I wore bell-bottoms, tie-dye shirts, and ponchos—even a pair of old coveralls. I, too, abjured drugs of any kind. But I had gone to the oth-er side of the world alone and was always eager for new adventures.

Will made something of a living selling stained glass panels and boxes. Since his expenses were so low at Monkeytop, he could get by without a regular salary. In the warmer months, we spent weekends at craft fairs ped-dling his work, or hiking, bike riding, and hanging out with other couples at Monkeytop. Will's van became our

camper if we wanted to spend a weekend at the coast.
There was a mattress in the back for sleeping. This was
never an ideal situation, but it became hellish when we
suffered an invasion of mosquitoes on the Outer Banks
and couldn't sleep for scratching bites and swatting at
the bedeviling insects.

In what I see now as a foolhardy adventure, we drove
that van all the way from North Carolina to Minnesota to
visit Will's mother, sleeping in it every night and washing
up at service stations along the way. I would suffer any
inconvenience for Will, and I would talk for both of us
by telling him stories of my work at the hospital or the
plots of books I was reading. He listened well and could
speak about one of my books as if he'd read it himself. I
didn't let myself think then about wanting more words
from him—words that would help me better understand
who he was and what he wanted from life. After all, I was
accustomed to a man like that.

Rather than using the VW bus to camp, I preferred
trips to the beach when the Monkeytop crowd rented
a house together. The women sunbathed nude, though
I couldn't bring myself to join them. I was still molded
by my Southern Baptist modesty. I complained to Will
that no one ever talked seriously about personal things
on these trips. It was all joking, quips, and small talk.
I was dying to spill my hopes and fears to one of the
Monkeytop women and become what I considered true
friends, bound by shared secrets and deep feelings.
Despite my attempts, it wasn't happening. They either
weren't receptive, or I didn't try hard enough.

I was an interloper, not one of the original dozen
who came together and formed the commune. I also
had replaced Will's former girlfriend, one of the twelve,
though she had moved on to another relationship by
then and didn't seem to resent me. She continued to

live at Monkeytop, so I saw her often. But I had a knack, from long habit, of marginalizing myself in a group of people, so I ended up with the familiar feeling of being lonely and isolated among the Monkeytoppers. It would become my life-long endeavor to conquer that feeling.

I remember the exact moment when I thought I was in love with Will. We were in my apartment on Airport Road in Chapel Hill, fresh off a bike ride. At some point, Will gently pushed me into the door of my refrigerator, pressed himself against me, and kissed me long and slow. I felt warmth flow down to my toes. This feeling must be love, I thought. I didn't know the difference between powerful physical attraction and love. All I knew was that it felt wonderful to be the object of affection, and I'll take more of that, please.

Will and I had talked about his wanting to up his game as a stained-glass artist. This would involve spending at least nine months in the United Kingdom studying and making stained glass at an art school there. Since we were in a committed relationship and wanted to be together, we both assumed I would go.

About eighteen months into our relationship, Will was accepted at that art school to study with Patrick Reyntiens, the leading stained glass artist in the UK. Reyntiens had restored, in collaboration with artist John Piper, the windows of the new Coventry Cathedral, which had been bombed during WWII. Reyntiens also taught at and ran an art school near High Wycombe, a large town about a thirty-minute train ride northwest of London. This was where we were headed. My desire to travel and see the world was insatiable. I loved Will, so I gave up my job, my apartment, my car, and all my possessions to go with him. By selling everything we each owned, we put together $10,000. We estimated it was enough at the time to see us through nine months in England.

A few weeks before we left for London, I moved into
Monkeytop with Will. Some of it was heady, some of it
fun, but ultimately, I was too private a person to embrace
communal life. I was always interested in new experiences and living at Monkeytop was an experience. Nightly
dinners around a huge old wooden wheel that served
as a dining table were a combination of jokes, laughter,
and sometimes debates. However, it was still the guys
who dominated, as in everything else.

Bands passing through Durham camped out in the
living room of the old house, prompting parties that
most of the area's tie-die crowd flocked to. At one cos-
tume party, a male friend came in his birthday suit. I was
amused by these parties, but was more bystander than
participant, taking in the wild wackiness of it all, not sure
where I fit in.

My parents were not happy about my living with Will,
"living in sin," the church called it. But I told my mother,
"At least we'll be living in sin in another country, so you
won't have to be embarrassed about it here at home."

This was small consolation to my mother, but she
knew it was pointless to try and dissuade me. Dad wasn't
pleased, either, but seemed to accept Will as part of my
life and related to him the way he always did with other men—never judging, but always joking and telling
stories.

We left Monkeytop for our great adventure in early
June of 1975, when the mornings were chilly for that
time of year. We boarded a plane for London by way of
Paris, where we spent a week knocking off the sights on
Will's tourist list. I was just as eager to see it all but wanted some down time to sit and sip a glass of wine at a
sidewalk café and watch the Parisians and the tourists
stroll by. It was hard to convince Will to take a break and
savor the place. He charged through museums ahead of

me when I wanted him to walk with me and discuss the paintings we were viewing. This reminded me of Dad's hyperactive way of going about tourist sights, and life—as if he were there but not there at the same time.

After the early flush of our romance, I began to bump up against our differences. Will was not one to be managed, though I sometimes tried to bend him to my wishes. We both had to make concessions. He was my first long-term relationship, and I had some learning to do.

Will and I hadn't bargained on housing in the UK being a challenge. For our first couple of weeks in High Wycombe, we rented a room over a pub and were starting to worry about finding permanent lodging. Then we met Pippa and John Ensdale, an English couple who liked us immediately. It was mutual. Since Pippa and John were leaving on holiday for two weeks, they offered us the use of their small house and the bounty of their backyard garden. While at Pippa and John's, Will and I continued to peruse the rental listings and soon learned that the English were reluctant to rent their homes because of the squatters movement of the '60s and '70s, in which hippies and the homeless (often the same) took over abandoned buildings and unoccupied houses for communes and refused to leave.

Once Pippa and John returned, they passed us on to another trusting couple to housesit while they were away. Eventually, we answered an ad for a semi-detached home on 34 Queen Street, High Wycombe, in a row of tidy two-story brick houses leading down to the railroad station and a thirty-minute train ride to London.

The older couple who had advertised the rental found us to be the perfect renters, since we were on a visa and would not be overstaying our welcome after they returned from visiting their children in Australia for a year.

We moved in the next month. I felt much more secure having found a house we could relax into for the next nine months. The one drawback for Yanks like us was that there was no central heat, only electric heaters, which the English called "electric fires." This was typical of homes throughout the country, I soon learned. When we traveled at the school holidays, we stayed in guesthouses and small inns. In those places, you had to put coins in a meter to have heat come on for an hour or two at a time. Having grown up a Southern hothouse violet, I struggled to adjust to a cold house at night and the unfortunate thrill of an icy toilet seat when I needed to use the bathroom in the small hours.

While Will was at the art school, I made my way to the London museums and read British authors such as Doris Lessing, Iris Murdoch, Anita Brookner, and Muriel Spark. These women kept me company when I was lonely for friends and family, much the way reading Charles Dickens when I was twelve assuaged the loneliness I felt at a new school.

At first, I thought that having complete freedom from the demands of a job would be liberating, but instead it was challenging to be okay with not being productive or earning a paycheck. Exercising my writing muscles could have been a satisfying way to fill some of the time, but I was resistant to it for reasons I couldn't explain. My mother wrote long newsy letters of home. I looked forward to her familiar handwriting on the airmail envelopes that would be pushed through the brass mail slot and land on the floor. Things seemed to be okay at home. Dad was working. He had installed a raised pen at the farm for quail and an enclosure in the woods with a wading pool for his mallard ducks. As was his custom, Dad left the writing to Mom. I doubt he sat still long enough to write a letter.

We bought an old Morris Minor auto, green with wooden sides, for a sum of four hundred pounds, and that gave me the liberty of driving around the country-side to small towns and villages in Buckinghamshire and beyond. The problem with the Morris was the fearsome stick shift and driving on the left side of the road. So I took driving lessons and mastered the manual transmission by the second lesson, finally banishing all remnants of Dad's assessment of my driving skills. Free at last from patriarchal judgment, I took to the Morris like a natural.

I used the car to visit old Norman churches in the area and make rubbings of their commemorative brass plaques. Usually found in the floors of the churches, they were sometimes quite large. These plaques might be of a knight or a lady and were created between the thirteenth and sixteenth centuries. Using a type of wax crayon called a heelball and paper akin to butcher paper, I made meticulous rubbings, putting the paper on top of the brass and bringing it to life by rubbing the heelball on top of the paper. Often, I talked with the vicar about the brasses and the history of the particular church I was in.

During a school break, Will and I visited a friend and her husband in Cambridge. This gave us the opportunity to get a brass rubbing of my most sought-after image: Sir Roger de Trumpington, the ultimate prized brass in England. Sir Roger was a knight in full armor, almost six feet tall, and lay in the Church of Saints Mary and Michael, located in the village of Trumpington near Cambridge. His image was said to be the second oldest brass in England.

Getting an image of Sir Roger was a big project, and Will agreed to help me. We toted our brass rubbing materials to the church on a mid-week morning. The church was an imposing structure, more Gothic than

Norman, made of stone with vaulted arches inside and delicate tracery in the large gothic window of the nave. The north chapel, where Sir Roger's brass lay, dated to the thirteenth century, the vicar told us. The rest of the church was fourteenth century and later. The vicar agreed to let us rub an image of Sir Roger, though he said it would soon be off-limits.

"Too many people doing it these days," he said. "Soon he'll be worn away."

I was glad to have made it under the wire. I wanted something to take home that would remind me of the age of the churches—a link to a distant past that gave me a comforting sense of continuity.

I started at Sir Roger's head and Will at his feet. The plan was to keep going until we met in the middle. I liked the feel of the heelball in my hand as the figure of Sir Roger began to emerge through the crisp white paper. I liked doing it with Will. I used black heelball, rubbing the knight's head with swift strokes. Soon I could make out his pointed, visored helmet. Sir Roger was a beauty. Will was getting the image of his feet, crossed at the ankles and resting against his loyal hound.

"Look at this—what we're doing," I said. "We're creating a masterpiece together."

"Yup—a good souvenir."

Inside, the air in the old church was chill and cave-like compared to the warmth outside. There was no sound except for the rasp-rasp of our chunky wax crayons dragging across the long scroll of paper. As I knelt on the cool stone floor to work on the brass, I thought about those who'd knelt in the same spot more than seven centuries before me.

Those stone floors and walls were eloquent in a way I hadn't anticipated. They had absorbed the prayers of long-ago supplicants and silently diffused them in the still, cool air. I knew that those earliest worshippers believed the earth was flat and that the sun revolved around it. Even so, I felt a kinship, having once shared with them a need to believe. These thoughts and feelings were like tender sprouts that might wither if exposed, so I didn't share them with Will. We didn't talk about things like that, and I didn't know much about his inner life. He was good with quips and jokes, like Dad. I was comfortable with Will because he felt familiar.

By that time, I had given up any religious beliefs I once held, like Dad had cast aside his Judaism, and considered myself an agnostic. I wasn't ready for atheism. My fundamentalist upbringing had left me feeling abused by religion, kept in line with threats of hell and damnation. None of it made sense to me, so I kept every belief system—and I'd explored a lot of them—at a distance. Yet, I wanted to keep the door ajar.

Getting an image of Sir Roger on paper was a workout. When the muscles of my forearms began to ache, I stood and stretched, told Will I was taking a break. "I'll join you later," he said, intent on the task at hand.

I left my heelball on the paper where it lay and walked alone through the thick wooden doors of the sanctuary, my footsteps echoing against the stones. The day outside was bright and unusually warm for Cambridgeshire. A breeze ruffled the leaves of a spreading oak, planted like a sentinel on the rise beside the church, as if guarding the ancient gravestones in the cemetery. Blinking in the sudden glare of sunlight, I made my way through the yard to the cemetery. Birds chattered, small banners of white clouds flapped against a deep blue sky.

I scanned the rows of gravestones, some listing at crazy angles, like crooked teeth. "Charlotte Weatherell, born May 22, 1824, died in childbirth, June 3, 1854 - her son James resting in her arms." Above the fading inscription

was carved a roundel encircling a small bird. Beside
Charlotte's grave were three smaller markers for Jane,
Lilly, and Tom Weatherell, all dead before their second
birthdays. "And he gathers the lamb into his arms," was
carved on Lilly's marker. Near Charlotte's stone was an
obelisk with the name Sarah Melton carved at its base,
"taken at sixteen to be with the Lord."

So much suffering. So much death. Was there meaning in being alive for such a short time?

I stood with head bowed. The sun was warm on my
back. The heat radiated from my back to the center of
my chest. It squeezed up my throat and suffused my face,
pushing out tears.

"I thought I'd come and see how you were getting
on."

I started. It was the vicar, his ruddy jowls folding softly
over his starched white Roman collar.

"I'm so moved reading these gravestones," I said. "It's
unutterably sad. All these children dead. Their mother
dying in childbirth at thirty, hardly older than I am."

"Ah, it's not so sad if you believe," said the vicar.

"But that's just it," I said, taking a deep breath. "I don't
believe in an afterlife. Life was so hard then. All they had
was their faith to keep them from going mad with grief
at these untimely deaths. I believe we made up a god to
assuage our fear of death. In our search for meaning, we
created God, not the other way around."

I had no hesitation in telling the vicar my take on religion. I'd been provocative in my debates with Dad, so
presenting an opposing view to a leader of the faithful
was not much of a leap. I wanted to see his reaction.

Instead of being shocked at my bold declaration of no
faith, the vicar was kind and patient.

"We all have periods of doubt," he said. "The ques-
tioning can make your faith stronger in the end."

As a child I had never questioned my faith, nor had I seen my parents examine theirs, unless you considered Dad's conversion an interrogation of his Judaism. It was a received truth, this faith, passed down through the generations of my mother's family—like family folk tales and legends—from parents to children and children to their children in turn.

Under the relentless radiance of the sun, the vicar's forehead beaded with sweat.

"Thank you for allowing me to come today, Vicar. You know, I did have a transcendent experience in there. But it was a reverence for all the people who came before me—not God."

"I hope you find your way," said the vicar. "A life without God can be a lonely one."

I was lonely when I had God, so letting go of God didn't change that.

"Thank you for speaking with me. Vicar. I've enjoyed our conversation."

And I had enjoyed talking with him. We had been discussing something deep and real, and I craved that kind of connection.

Then the kind man turned and went back into the church. What must he have made of me?

I returned to the north chapel, Will, and Sir Roger. Will was almost to the knight's waist. I joined him at our task.

Though the vicar was a compassionate man, I didn't need his consolation. I was done with easy answers and platitudes. I'd already seen enough of the dark side of life in my work—holding the hand of a teenaged boy dying of cancer, consoling a wife whose husband had tried to kill himself by shooting a pistol through the roof of his mouth (and lived with only a partial brain), and telling a young husband that his wife had died after a routine procedure. During my years as a social worker, Dad's incapacitating pain and my work life were all consuming, and I had no sanctuary. I was constantly primed for some terrible illness to strike me or the ones I loved. The year in England was supposed to help me figure out what to do next.

## 37

While we were in England, a piece of what to do next involved Will. One day in late winter, we'd been arguing heatedly, and, as usual, couldn't work out a resolution. We didn't know how to fight productively. Instead, we usually walked away from each other to cool off. Shortly after this particular argument, Will found me in another room with my back to him. He turned me by the shoulders to face him, and said, "Let's get married."

His proposal ambushed me. I was still fuming over whatever we had been fighting about. I thought it odd that Will talked marriage on the heels of a row, but I nevertheless agreed on the spot, despite my deeply conflicted feelings about marriage. Marrying Will seemed so much like the next logical step that it overrode any qualms I might have had. I had yet to learn to pay attention to my gut, which may have been telling me otherwise. Didn't all couples fight occasionally? Didn't we love each other? I was unmoored in a country not my own and with no job. The certainty of knowing what would happen next was a comfort.

We called our parents to say that we were engaged and would get married soon after our return to the United States. Our respective parents accepted the news graciously. Perhaps they, too, thought the marriage inevitable.

My agreeing to marry Will was a turnaround for me. As a teen, I had vowed that I would never marry, that

I wanted a career. By the end of college, the marriage virus had claimed several of my girlfriends, but I was still adamant about not succumbing myself.

A few years out in the world on my own tamed me, and I began to wonder if, and whom, I might marry. What I sought was a deep emotional bond—the thing I had been denied growing up.

The wedding on May 22, 1975, two months after we arrived home, was small and on the cheap. We had an unusual guest list of hippie friends from Monkeytop along with church ladies who were friends of my parents and had known me growing up. I didn't necessarily want a traditional wedding in our church, but I yielded to my mother's wishes to avoid a struggle and to make her happy.

In the vestibule of West Main Baptist, I waited with Dad, in his omnipresent crew cut and his only suit. I wore an ivory gown that flowed from a big collar. I bought it not because I loved it or looked great in it, but because it was a bargain—forty dollars for a dress from a sample sale at Harrods in London. The lessons learned in Belk's bargain basement with my mother were still with me.

Dad moved from foot to foot, not saying much, but definitely conveying a sense of "let's just get this bit over with."

He glanced at my bouquet, which included baby's breath, its white flowers so tiny and fragile that a whisper would make them shudder.

"Hey, Cruella, look at those flowers," he whispered. "You must be nervous to make them jiggle like that. Looks as though they're animated." He laughed.

If I had been waiting for him to say something sweet— that he loved me, that I looked beautiful, that he was sad to have to give me away but wished the best for this marriage—I should have known better. Teasing was his substitute for just about any emotion except anger. I felt tears invading and fought them back.

On his arm, after the organ started playing a Bach cantata, I walked to the altar and to Will. My sisters, who were my bridesmaids, said later that I looked as though I was going to my funeral.

Years afterward, as I thought about Dad's teasing, I understood that it fit his pattern of making fun of things in order to avoid feelings. He had made light of my childhood illnesses, cuts, and scrapes, even surgery. At those times, I found his jokiness reassuring. On my wedding day, his teasing only seemed callous. I still craved his empathy and approval.

After the ceremony, my parents hosted a reception at Danville's Wednesday Club. No dancing or alcohol. It was a staid affair. Since we had no money and had been away for almost a year, Will and I decided to spend our wedding night at the lake house. Several Monkeytop friends accompanied us. They camped in the area and partied with us by the lake.

Afterward, when Will and I were alone, I felt awkward. Sleeping with him that night in my parents' bed felt incestuous. I wanted to run.

I didn't, because I felt bound to make a good marriage with Will.

What I didn't know or understand at the time was that I kept seeking in men the same emotional traits that were my father's. I joked that if you put me in a roomful of men, I would be drawn to the one who was most emotionally unavailable. On the surface, Will was the opposite of my father, but underneath, there were similarities.

# 38

The first two years of our marriage were fairly calm and happy enough. Then Will got the baby bug after hearing one of his friends wax eloquent about watching the birth of his daughter. While I didn't feel a desperate need to be a parent—something I told Will before we were married—I agreed to get pregnant. I didn't want to withhold from Will the thing he seemed to want most, but I was apprehensive, since my role models for parenting weren't the best. I'd been on the pill and knew that it might take months to get pregnant, so I figured I'd have time to get used to the idea. I got pregnant that first month after stopping the pill.

Will and I were stunned when an ultrasound at twenty-six weeks revealed two bodies and two heartbeats. Since our babies' heads were together at the bottom of my uterus, Will said, "They might be Siamese twins." At first I thought he was joking, but he was serious.

"I'm not the least bit worried about them being Siamese twins," I replied. "Look up the odds of having Siamese twins—they're astronomical."

"But I saw on the ultrasound that their heads were touching."

"And at the next ultrasound, they'll probably be in a different position."

Nothing I said could assuage Will's fears of an abnormal birth. He talked about it frequently and even consulted a doctor he knew. The doctor's reassurance didn't help. Will was convinced we were having Siamese twins. His harping on what I considered a ridiculous notion undermined my peace of mind when what I really needed was support. I was carrying two babies, and I had to take care of him at the same time, reassuring him that everything was going to be fine. It should have been the other way around.

Instead of conjoined twins, my doctor was concerned about my delivering too early. In my last trimester, she put me on six weeks' bed rest to ensure my babies stayed where they were until nature prepared them to come into the world. Six weeks dragged on without much company but our two cats, who slept near me. To pass the time, I read books, always a need and a pleasure, even more so during my confinement. My parents didn't visit, nor did they offer to help. I knew my mother had her hands full with Dad and didn't have much left over to give to me. Dad seemed to be declining even more. Though I understood the reasons for my parents' lack of support, I felt lonely and abandoned at a time when I needed my mother as I approached motherhood myself.

Will spent his days working at his stained-glass studio, then came home and cooked dinner. By this time, he was getting commissioned work for homes, businesses, and a church. He supplemented what he earned through commissions by teaching classes in designing and fabricating stained glass. This provided an income that supported us temporarily without my paycheck.

I was protective of the babies I was carrying, to the point that I ate only the most wholesome fresh foods I could find, drank nothing but milk and water, and decided that I would have a natural childbirth. The latter was a big mistake. When I went into labor, the pain was fiercer than anything I'd experienced or anticipated. Will and I had taken a Lamaze class, but he was so stressed

*The author at seven months pregnant with identical twins.*

and excited when the time came that he forgot to coach me on the breathing technique. Instead, between contractions, I coached him to coach me.

Once in the delivery room, while I was laboring with every muscle I commanded, I watched the progression of my struggle in a mirror over my head. I glimpsed my first son crown and then felt the rest of his tiny body slide from my birth canal into the waiting hands of the physician and nurses. I was exhausted when the doctor told me to start pushing again. Only the threat of having my second son by Caesarian motivated me to keep working. My second son was born face up—or sunny-side-up as the nurses joked—and the pain was more intense because the back of his head was pressing against my spine. By the end of my labor, I was exhausted but euphoric and proud that I had produced two healthy boys, so happy and pumped up on endorphins that I didn't sleep at all the night after. We named them Drew and Max, and I was in love.

My doctor told me that my sons shared the same placenta and outer membrane, called the chorion, so they were identical twins. It was a few months before we realized they were also mirror twins—one right-handed, the other left, matching tiny moles on opposite sides of their bodies. It was both freakish and miraculous. I worried that they might have trouble differentiating from each other as they grew. A twin bond can be so

*The author
with her
newborn sons.
Drew weighed
5 pounds, 5
ounces, and
Max was 5
pounds, 11
ounces.*

strong it excludes others. That was not the case with Max and Drew. They were close in a fractious way. After they learned to talk, Drew said the world was not big enough for both him and his brother. One of them would have to go, and it would be Max.

I confused them only once after their birth, when a nurse brought in Drew to be nursed, took him away, and then returned with Max. I asked if she'd made a mistake and brought me the same baby twice. Fortunately, they were wearing their baby bracelets for identification. After that, I never confused the two again.

When I got home from the hospital, my mother came for a couple of days to help. She was there for my sons, whom she liked to hold and rock. That was the fun part. Even that wasn't enough to keep her more than overnight. "I have to get back to your father," she said. I didn't doubt that was true, but I wanted her to stay longer. I needed her, terrified as I was of being left alone to cope.

Fortunately, Will's mother came and stayed for a couple of weeks, which was a godsend for both of us. She cooked our meals, cleaned, and was hands-on with whatever we needed. Before she left, I begged her to stay longer, too.

Like all new mothers, I was both elated and overwhelmed. While I had an intense love and desire to nurture and protect my boys, my emotional life became more complicated. I hit a wall of post-partum depression, feeling that life as I knew it was over, and that was mostly true.

Exhaustion from lack of sleep and feeling that I was always on my back nursing a babe or two made me feel trapped. At my first follow-up doctor visits, when asked how I was doing, I wept. I didn't have enough milk for both babies, and I had to supplement with formula. When he was home, Will helped as much as he could, changing diapers and bottle-feeding our boys their formula. They were colicky infants, so Will and I sat side by side in front of the TV and each rocked one wailing boy night after night for several weeks, soothing them, patting their backs, and waiting for them to calm down so we could all go to sleep.

Finally, someone suggested I switch over to only formula so that Will could help out more with feedings. That switch, at around four months, helped lift my mood. Somehow, I made it through the worst of the depression. There was no time for feeding the depression when I was feeding two infants.

Friends visited, eager to see the babies. "How can you tell them apart?" they asked.

"It's easy for us, because we're with them all the time and can see their subtle differences," I said.

Random people I met, when out with my sons, scolded me for not dressing them alike, as if there were some commandment that twins should be wearing identical clothes. My response was, "I don't dress them alike, because they're two different individuals, each with his own identity." I wanted my sons to grow up knowing that each was appreciated for who he was and not lumped into being one of a duo. I chided my family for referring to my boys as "the twins."

When Drew and Max were about six weeks old, Will and I drove to the coast to share a beach rental with the rest of my family. This was the first time Dad met my sons. While my mother and siblings cooed over our boys, Dad was detached. I thought bringing grandsons into Dad's life might make him perk up and encourage him to be on hand to teach the next generation how to fish. At my insistence, he agreed to hold Drew, and I gingerly placed my boy in his arms. Almost immediately, Dad gave Drew back to me, as if he were a tiny space alien. This felt like a gut punch. Dad was unreachable. He seemed dead inside. I wanted to wail, "What is wrong with you?"

≈≈≈≈ 39 ≈≈≈≈

After my sons made their appearance, Dad became a professional hospital patient with chronic and disabling back pain. He ricocheted from Danville Memorial Hospital to Duke Hospital, to Baptist Hospital in Winston Salem, and to the Veterans Administration Hospital in Durham, all in the space of a couple of years. At each, his doctors eventually got fed up and discharged him with no suggestions for follow-up that I knew of.

In the beginning of his troubles, he worked as much as he was able, but working always ended in another bout of pain and hospitalization. He metamorphosed into an invalid, not even leaving the bed to use the bathroom. He threatened to use one of his guns on himself. My mother removed his hunting rifles and the German Luger he brought back from the war and gave them to one of Dad's hunting buddies for safekeeping.

When I visited, just walking into Dad's room would be like setting off a pre-recorded tape that played in an endless loop.

"Hi Dad, I'm glad to see you."

"I've had a rough week with my back. I can't even get out of bed. I'm telling you I need to go back into the hospital."

"But Dad, you've been in three hospitals already, and they did nothing for you. Why don't you try getting up and going to physical therapy again? Maybe a new therapist."

"It doesn't work. I don't need physical therapy. I need relief from this pain."

Had I told him I had terminal cancer, he would not have skipped a beat in his litany of pain. I wondered if the manifestation of physical pain might be a cover for emotional pain that he would never acknowledge. Was there something he had carried from his WWII experiences? Was he conflicted about the choice he made to renounce his birth religion and Jewish identity?

I couldn't let go of feeling responsible for him, of trying to reach him. Our relationship had once been so simple and straightforward. He was the father. I was the daughter. He took care of me. At some point that flipped, and I took on the impossible task of crossing the moat and breaching the walls of his fortified castle.

Jane remembered that Dad had been under the care of a psychiatrist when he was at Baptist Hospital and that I had talked to his doctors. I understood by then that there were few, if any, effective treatments for severe depression. The subject of Dad having electroconvulsive therapy, as Grandma Sadye had endured multiple times, never came up, though perhaps it should have.

Visiting him became a duty that I dreaded. I felt helpless and unable to make contact, except as a sounding board for his complaints. He begged me to get him into the VA in Durham, so I did the paperwork to have him taken there.

The VA's green-tiled hallways smelled of disinfectant and unwashed bodies. I opened the door to Dad's room and steeled myself to go in. It was furnished with a bed, a side table, and a TV. The shade was drawn against the late afternoon sun, and the room was dim in contrast to the brightness outside. A sour smell assaulted my nostrils. He was supine in the bed, as usual, an inert lump under the thin hospital sheet. I doubted he'd showered for days.

He hadn't shaved for days, either. A graying stubble blanketed the lower half of his face, as if competing for attention with his crew cut now in its in-between stage. Tufts of hair grew at the edges of his bald spot, making him look like an old barn owl. His cheeks were concave, with only the full, rounded lips serving as an incongruous reminder of bygone youth and good health.

A white Styrofoam pitcher and a water glass with its curved straw sat on the bedside table. Dad's hands and arms lay on top of the sheet, by his sides. On the ring finger of his right hand was his red and gold Masonic ring, on the left, his wedding band. Both rings loosely encircled the fingers of hands that once wielded a dentist's drill, grasped a pair of forceps, steered our motorboat as it pulled me on a pair of skis, or passed a collection tray at a Sunday church service. Now they lay motionless and pale on top of the sheet.

The intelligent hazel eyes were there, but focused on some middle distance, neither looking around him nor directly at me.

"Hi Pops," I chirped with fake cheeriness. "How are you today?"

"Not good. I had to get the nurse to hold my water glass to give me a sip of water. Reaching for the glass sets off muscle spasms in my back. I knew I shouldn't have tried to walk today. That just irritated my back further. That physical therapist doesn't know what he's talking about. I need to stay flat until these spasms ease off."

On hearing this, I crumpled inside.

"I'm sorry you had such a rough day, but don't you think being so inactive will make it harder to get your back muscles in shape?"

His eyes darted to the game show flashing soundlessly on the wall-mounted television.

"I don't see how I can get up. I'm telling you, I'm

hurting bad. They had me on this exercise regimen, and it made things worse."

He continued to stare at the TV screen.

"Listen, Dad, the TV reminds me, did you watch that program I told you about, the one where Max and Drew are featured as they're learning to walk? The American Dance Festival—you know, the place where I'm working—created the video. They wanted to demonstrate movement from the beginning, when a child first starts lurching about. It was hilarious to watch."

"I guess I forgot," he said tonelessly, still staring at the TV.

"Would you like me to bring Drew and Max the next time I come? They're entertaining at this age."

"Yeah, sure. But I don't know what I'm going to do if they try to get me up tomorrow. Maybe you can call Dr. Pittman at Duke, see if he'll take me. They're not doing anything for me here."

This was the same Dr. Pittman who had once called me Miss Kissoff a few years earlier when I was a medical social worker.

I sighed, releasing my clenched jaw.

"You remember—Dr. Pittman didn't help you before when you were in Duke. You got fed up with him, too. Dad, you have to get well. You promised to take the boys fishing," I pleaded.

No response.

"Well, okay, I've got to go, Dad. I'll see you in a few days."

If he heard what I said, he didn't acknowledge it. I bent down to kiss his stubbled cheek and gave him a pat on the shoulder before walking out.

As I slipped past other patients' rooms on the way to the elevator, I felt rage. If Dad refused to do anything about getting better, then why didn't he just do away with himself? He'd threatened it often enough. I punched the black elevator button and was immediately ashamed of myself for thinking this. But anger kept the thought alive. His hopelessness had gotten to me. He was always the strong, optimistic one—converting to Christianity and marrying out of his faith; going to undergraduate and dental school while having a wife and child to support; buying land and building his own dental office on it; buying four lots at Smith Mountain lake, knowing the land value would appreciate; buying the farm he always wanted and building his dream home on it. He saw no obstacles, only opportunities. Now I pondered—who was the shrunken fifty-four-year-old man in the hospital bed, enfeebled long before his time? And why was he hell-bent on a slow, creeping self-destruction? His spirit seemed dead already. I couldn't reach him. I felt like a failure.

The VA doctors did not meet Dad's expectations, nor he theirs, so they discharged him after a few days. He landed back home, no better for the latest hospitalization. He was on a number of medications that included self-prescribed muscle relaxants and painkillers, until finally, his pharmacist put an end to it and only filled prescriptions written by his doctors.

I was away from home during Dad's declining years, and it was difficult to get a complete picture of what was going on. The facts were filtered through my mother. I thought there was much she wasn't telling me.

In March 1980, Grandpa Herman died—a heart attack at home. He was eighty-eight years old. His sudden death ambushed me. I had thought of him as nearly immortal and knew the world would be a less interesting and lonelier place without him.

Because my life was a round of work, children, husband, and Dad, I hadn't the space to mourn Grandpa in the way he deserved.

Dad was in Baptist Hospital at the time of Grandpa's death, so Mom made the arrangements for Grandpa's body to be shipped to Danville for burial. My sister Jane and her husband flew to New York to bring Grandma Sadye back to live in the Roman Eagle nursing home in Danville, thought to be one of the best in the area at the time. Dad had wanted Grandma Sadye to live with him and my mother. Mom was adamant that she was not taking care of another Kossoff. Who could blame her?

At the time, I was not aware of Mom's plans for Grandpa. Against Jewish tradition, Grandpa's body was embalmed, and he was buried in the family plot in a Christian service.

The pastor from my parents' church presided at the small service at Wrenn-Yeatts Funeral Home in Danville, with Dad and Grandma Sadye present. Jane and I were there because we lived closer to Danville. Roger, in Florida, and Mary, in Northern Virginia, did not make the trip for the funeral. I have little memory of the service other than anger and incredulity at Mom's show of disrespect for Grandpa's heritage. How could she arrange a Christian burial for her Jewish father-in-law? What did Dad think of this? Was he so far gone that he didn't know what she was doing or care? And why did she do it? For convenience or for having the last word?

Had I known what she was planning, I would have intervened. There were two synagogues in Danville at the time, and I could have consulted with one or both of the rabbis.

No one sat shiva for Grandpa. No Hebrew words were spoken at his service: *Baruch atah Adonai, Dayan Ha-Emet. Blessed are You, Adonai, Truthful Judge; Adonai natan, Adonai lakach, yehi shem Adonai m'vorach. God has given, God has taken away, blessed be the name of God.*

The shame of having tried to convert Grandpa when I

was a child never left me. Now the shame was multiplied tenfold by a burial service that Grandpa would have hated. Grandma Sadye, in shock at Grandpa's sudden death, was not truly aware of what was going on.

Dad fell back into his pain and his bed after rousing himself to attend his father's funeral. If he mourned the death of his father, he never spoke about it.

Six months after Grandpa Herman's death, Dad entered the University of Virginia Hospital in Charlottesville. He had threatened suicide enough that he was put on the psychiatric unit under twenty-four-hour suicide watch. Finally, the doctors focused on his mental and emotional state. They wanted to referee a meeting between Mom and Dad to try and understand the dynamic between them and get them to talk to each other. My mother was like Dad in that she never talked about anything remotely resembling a feeling. Although she dreaded the visit with the doctors, she dutifully complied. But she didn't want to go alone. Whether she asked one of my siblings first, I don't know, but she asked me and I agreed. It would mean rearranging my work schedule at the American Dance Festival and finding additional childcare for Max and Drew.

Mom drove us to Charlottesville because she would never ride with me. I assumed it was because she wanted to be in control, at least in that aspect of her life.

We were both keyed up when we arrived at the hospital for the meeting with Dad's doctors. They told us they were having a hard time getting through to him and that perhaps he would open up a bit to Mom.

Not very likely, I thought to myself.

I stayed in the waiting room, reading to distract myself until the session was over. When Mom appeared, she looked drained and told me that Dad wouldn't say much. The session had been a bust.

We went into Dad's room on the psych wing. Dad lay on his back in the bed, picking at the sheets. The sour odor of his sweat and unwashed body permeated the room. His forehead had an oily sheen.

He launched his boat of woes even as we were trying to drift in another direction.

"Jean," he said to me, "you've got to get me out of here." It was more of an order than a plea. "I can't take it in this place. They've done nothing for me." He didn't look directly at me, but at the wall across from his bed.

"Dad, in the last two years, you've been in at least four hospitals, and you say the same thing at every place."

"I want you to get me back into the VA in Durham."

Here we go again, I thought. I was frustrated, angry, and weary of the months of visiting him in hospitals, trying to cheer him up the way he had cheered me when I was a kid.

"When you were at the VA, all you wanted was to get out. You said they didn't help you there, either. I can't do this, Dad."

"Yes you can." He twisted the sheet in his right hand.

I wanted to make things different, make him whole again, but he was beyond reasoning with, and I felt helpless. A surge of anger heated up my spine. We had played out this scene many times before.

"I love you, Dad," I said, "But I can't let you manipulate me anymore." And I walked out of his room, my heart banging hard against my ribs and my whole body shaking.

# ⁂⁂⁂ 41 ⁂⁂⁂

A week after the UVA Hospital visit, I pulled into our driveway with two bags of groceries in the back of my station wagon. I gathered the groceries and paused at the back door, waiting for Will to come help. He didn't. I cradled one of the bags under my left arm and stooped to turn the doorknob with my right hand. When I walked into the kitchen, Will was standing in the hallway door. It was quiet in the house. The boys must be napping, I thought.

Will slouched against the doorframe. I was annoyed that he hadn't come to help me and then alarmed.

"What is it?" I asked.

"I have some bad news," Will's face was still expressionless. "Your sister called. Your father's dead. He hung himself."

"What?"

I dropped the groceries, one bag spilling an avocado and apples that rolled across the floor.

"But that can't be. He was on twenty-four-hour suicide watch."

"He tied the sash of his bathrobe around his neck and looped the other end around the hook on the bathroom door. That's what your sister said."

I had seen that hook when my mother and I visited. It was less than six feet—my father's height—from the floor.

He must have sagged against the loop as he sat on

the floor. At any time, he could have moved or stood to release the pressure.

The brutality of that image unnerved me. My hands started shaking. I clasped them together. I didn't cry.

Dad had threatened often to kill himself. He said his physical pain was too much to bear.

Will began to scoop up the groceries from the floor. I heard Drew and Max waking from their naps, but it didn't fully register.

I phoned my mother's house. My sister Jane picked up. She told me that the other family members knew. I told her I was on my way. I called the bus station for the schedule. A bus would leave Durham for Danville in an hour. I threw some clothes, a toothbrush, a hairbrush, underwear into a bag.

Will packed our sons into their car seats and dropped me at the bus station. He told me to take care and that he would see me soon. I was relieved to be alone, to have time away from parenting to think, to grieve.

The bus followed the familiar highway, Route 86 North. I had driven it many times, as recently as the previous week. The lowering sun slanted across the grimy bus window. I watched the farms with their harvested fields slide by. There were yellow stalks where rows of tobacco stood earlier. Other fields were only stubble. It was October 1, 1980, and a foreboding of fall was in the air. The bus passed a vacant two-story farmhouse set back in a field with a large tree sheltering one side. I always looked for it on 86, to see if it was still standing. Its sightless windows reminded me of abandonment.

※※※※※

Dad's casket sat on its bier at the front of Danville's West Main Baptist Church, where he had been a deacon. We were alone with him—my mother, Roger, and Jane. Mary said she didn't want to remember him in death, so she stayed away. My mother caressed his face, bent down to kiss him. "Oh, Hugh," she cried. She began to sob, and I embraced her. Jane and Roger huddled close.

The funeral wreaths on stands around the casket had a sickly sweet smell, almost nauseating. Their blossoms were pale, waxy—like his skin.

"Dad, what have you done?" I whispered. I touched his hands. They were hard and cold, like marble.

My father's face was both familiar and strange. His signature graying crew cut above a receding hairline was there, his surgically shortened nose, fleshy lips, and the full eyebrows that met in a point in the middle—like mine. His hazel eyes were hidden beneath the stitched-closed lids.

He'd been dressed in a dark suit and tie, garb he reserved only for church services and important occasions. I couldn't see his neck, where the ligature marks might be. I saw my father frozen in mid-life and I saw something else—a prominent red mark in the center of his forehead.

I stared at that red mark. Was it a bruise or a ruptured blood vessel from the hanging? I knew that petechiae—purple or red spots caused by bleeding from broken capillary blood vessels—often appear on the skin of those who've died from strangulation. I tried to look through the makeup for other spots. I only saw the one, alien and mysterious.

I looked at my once-vibrant father, the one who joked and teased and played checkers with me when I was young, the strong, invincible man of my childhood, the man I somehow lost over the years. I couldn't believe that his restless soul was quieted, that he would never get to know his grandsons, or that I would never be able to wring out of him the answers I sought.

I hoped he was at peace, but I feared he had simply ceased to exist. There was a heartbreaking finality to that thought. I wanted there to be a heaven where he would be waiting for me someday, but I didn't believe it. I took no comfort from it.

Roger told us later that he saw the coroner's photographs, and that in them, Dad was slumped against the bathroom door, the bathrobe sash still noosed around his neck, his eyes open. What must he have been thinking in those last moments?

❦❦❦❦❦

A few days after the funeral, my mother phoned, distraught. "The newspaper has a front-page story about Daddy's suicide. One of Daddy's former patients wrote it. How could he?" Her voice shook with emotion.

"Mom, it's okay. A lot of people knew about Dad's decline. You know how small towns are."

But my mother, whose reputation in town and in her church was paramount to her, would not be consoled.

"I just can't believe it. How will I look people in the eye?"

"There's nothing to be ashamed of. Suicides are more common than we know. People need to understand it better." At the same time, my heart sank, because I knew my mother was right about Danville.

"Your father's reputation is ruined."

"His patients will always remember him with fondness. Suicide can't take that away. He'll always be the man that his fishing and hunting buddies loved." I felt as if I was speaking a language she didn't understand. "Mom, I'm so sorry. I wish this hadn't happened."

This must be what she needed to hear from me. She said goodbye. Were my words of comfort enough? Did she call Jane or Mary?

❧❧❧❧❧

The aftermath of Dad's death was as painful as his death itself. My mother told me sometime later, "I would never have said what you said or walked out on my father like that." She must have told my sisters and brother what had happened at that last visit. There was an accusatory letter from one of my siblings. The family gatherings we had after Dad's death were glum and silent.

"What did you say to him?" one family member asked.

I had no defense. The question stung and reverberated over the years. It made me angry and alienated me from my family.

The burden of Dad's demands had fallen on me, even though I had a family of my own to care for. Mom was exhausted. Mary and Roger lived far enough away to be unavailable. Jane was devoted, but as the youngest, she was closest to our mother and supported her.

My anger was a cover for the despair I felt at being scapegoated, even though I'd done my best to save Dad from himself.

I became guarded around them. If I let them see how I was suffering, they might pile on. But my grief was also linked to shame. Had I somehow contributed to his unraveling?

❧❧❧❧❧

In the ensuing years, I dreamt about my father a lot. I would see him across the street as I was walking somewhere and call out to him, only to watch him disappear around a corner. I would spot him in a car driving in the opposite direction, and when I turned to look, the car would be gone. In the most disturbing dream, I sat beside him on a bench and offered him my new baby girl to hold. He took the baby and broke her neck.

⊰⊱⊰⊱⊰⊱

I was overwhelmed by the demands of my job, my young toddlers, my husband, and my own processing of Dad's death. While I wanted to be a comfort to my mother, I didn't have the emotional reserves to be present for her. I felt guilty about this—that I was letting everyone down. I began to fall into my own dark rabbit hole.

My guilt and grief turned inward, and my simmering depression boiled over into a deep and incapacitating desolation. Two weeks after Dad's funeral, my mother-in-law came to help out with my sons.

One evening when she had made dinner, and I was lying in bed crying, she called me to the table. "I'm not hungry, thank you." I said.

That simple statement apparently triggered her: She stalked into the bedroom and stood by the bed, hands on hips, and spat out the words, "If you don't get up out of that bed and be a good wife to your husband, I will take these children from you."

I was shocked into speechlessness. She had attacked me when I was so far down, I didn't have the energy to defend myself—nor would I have done so, because she was Will's mother.

Will must have complained to her. I felt betrayed and angry, and I told him so that night after his mother and the boys had gone to bed, when he came into our bedroom. The nearest thing at hand was my sewing basket, so I reached in and started lobbing spools of thread at him.

"How could you betray me to your mother?" Spool of thread, ducking.

"You married me for better or worse." Spool of thread hit target on arm.

"How could you be so callous and unsupportive at a time when I needed you most?" Spool of thread hit wall.

"Your mother threatened to take the boys away from me. How cruel could she be?"

"I'm sorry," Will said.

But sorry wasn't enough.

I wanted him to defend me to his mother, but I knew that was too much to ask. Will avoided confrontations, and his mother was imperious. Eventually she left for her home in Minnesota, and I forced myself back to work at the American Dance Festival and to holding up my end of parenting and housekeeping, but recovery was long and difficult.

Added to my guilt about my father was my shame at not being there emotionally for my sons, who were fourteen months old. Will was a grown-up who was capable of understanding what was happening to me. My sons were innocents caught in a family tragedy, and they would never know their grandfather or go fishing with him as I did as a child. It broke my heart.

## 42

A month after Dad's death, my mother talked with her lawyer, a longtime family friend, about suing UVA Medical Center for negligence. He advised against it.

His reasons, as my mother relayed them, were that she wouldn't want to go through a lengthy trial. Nor would she want what was in the medical records to be made public. This statement caught my attention. I desperately wanted to know what was in those medical records.

My mother would not grant me access to them. She told me they were Dad's private business, and I had no reason to go snooping around. Her resistance only honed my determination to get to the bottom of whatever I thought she was hiding. I knew Dad had been acting out against her. Had he lashed out both at her and the path he had chosen, the one that led him away from his Jewish roots? Did he regret his marriage and conversion?

I phoned Dad's chief psychiatrist at UVA Hospital. He told me Dad was the most difficult patient he'd ever had. He said he was unable to get near the source of Dad's deep despair. When I heard this, I hurt for Dad. He must have been so lonely, unable to share any part of himself with anyone. The psychiatrist's words should have relieved me of feeling the burden of Dad's suicide. Rationally, I understood that if professionals couldn't get through to him, then my not getting through to him most of my life was not my fault. That was true, but it was hard to expunge the guilt and feelings of not being good enough that had become ingrained in me since childhood.

# 43

Five weeks after Dad's funeral, I bypassed my mother and spoke directly to her lawyer. Obstacles, such as Mom, had always been roadblocks that I found a way to drive around to get what I wanted. The lawyer suggested I come to his office.

His practice was located in the brick Law Building on Patton Street. I entered an office weighty with brown leather chairs, dark wood paneling, and bookcases filled with law books.

He welcomed me, an unlit pipe dangling from the right corner of his mouth, and motioned for me to sit as he eased into a high-back leather desk chair.

"Why do you want to see these records?" he asked.

"Because I want to understand my father and why he committed suicide."

"He did it because he was in terrible back pain," the lawyer said.

"I think there was more to it than that, and I want to see if there are things in those medical records that will help explain why my father let chronic pain defeat him when others live with it."

"You know your father had an affair."

This revelation came as a blow, and I flinched inside, like an electrical zap had gone off in my guts. This was not something I had ever expected to hear about my father.

I was too shocked to ask how he knew this intimate information about Dad. They were friends, yes, but would Dad have confided in him?

I sat silent and stared at the lawyer's bookshelves.

From the corner of my eye, I saw that he lit his pipe and was pulling the air through it with a soft pop-pop sound—the sound I knew so well from my father drawing on his pipe.

"But how could he? And with whom?"

"One of his dental assistants."

The idea of Dad sleeping with a dental assistant was more like tabloid fodder than something I ever thought my father capable of. I wanted to spare my mother this knowledge. I swore this was a secret I would never divulge to her. She'd been hurt enough. It never occurred to me that she might have already known.

My heart pounded and my hands shook as I waited for the lawyer's reply.

He steepled his fingertips and leaned back in the chair, eyes staring past me. The chair creaked as he shifted his weight. The slanting late afternoon sun cast a pall over the room, putting much of it in shadow.

After what seemed like an eternity, he said, "I'll let you see the records."

He stood, went to a file drawer, and pulled out a folder. "Follow me," he said.

The lawyer ushered me to an empty office nearby, turned on the overhead fluorescent lights, and told me to take a seat behind a clean desk. He dropped the file on the desktop and pushed it toward me.

"You can only look at them here," he cautioned. "You cannot make copies or bring anything with you. Take your time. I'll be in my office if you need anything."

With the detachment of a doctor learning about a new

patient, I pulled my chair under the desk and opened the brown folder. I learned that from Dad—not to feel anything. In situations where others get emotional and break down, I have vast reserves of psychic Novocain. Only an interior adrenaline buzz lets me know something emotional is going on. Much later, the real feelings surface, in private.

Hand-scrawled notes, from residents, nurses, and physical therapists, marked the passing of each day of Dad's waning life.

The psychiatric resident wrote, "A difficult patient, obsessed with control and unable to gain insight about his condition."

A nurse's entry marked August 25, 1980, observed, "The patient was crying. He seems to have regular crying spells, but when I asked him about it, he replied, 'a man doesn't cry; I've never cried.'"

Someone else wrote that in a rare unguarded moment my father admitted to sabotaging his therapy and suggested that maybe he really didn't want to get well.

The resident reappeared, quoting my father in a fit of pique at being pressed to talk: "If I have to talk about feelings again, I'll vomit. Feelings are the wind, the woods, the water, times when I'm out of doors. They don't have anything to do with people."

This hit me hard. Had he never had feelings for me?

I shared that love of nature and the outdoors with my father—his gift to me. My fondest memories were of fishing with him at Nags Head and clinging to his back as we rode the ocean swells, of swimming and water skiing at Smith Mountain Lake. I knew that he had hunted and fished as a teenager, long before he met my mother. It was what distinguished him from his intellectual father, my Grandpa Herman. Dad didn't fit the profile of his urban Jewish kin. Had he felt an outsider with his family as I did with mine? Is that why he sought the opposite of what he'd grown up with?

My father's voice, as revealed in the chart notes, was not the voice of a man who wanted to die only because of physical pain. The notes revealed there was pain from a much deeper place in his psyche. He denied having any feelings for people, which included his family. He was a man obsessed with control. The records confirmed my suspicions that physical pain was not the only reason for Dad's suicide, but I felt no sense of vindication—only a deep sadness. And I was none the wiser about why he did it. I had been clutching at air.

At some level, my mother must have been relieved at Dad's death. For several years, she'd had to live with a man she no longer recognized, a man she couldn't help, a man who turned against her.

Of course she grieved, but she was also free. I, too, felt relief, for I knew Dad had slipped through our fingers and gone to a dark place from which he had no wish to return. Death released him from that place.

❧❧❧❧❧

Years after Dad's death, I learned that he carried a hip flask of whiskey that he offered to Will in private when we visited. I found out my mother had known about the affair, because she washed the sheets and towels he brought home from the lakeside cottage where he had his trysts. She kept it a secret for twenty years after his death, only sharing the information the year she was dying. I couldn't work out how he was capable of an affair when he complained of back pain all the time. How did he manage to be someone's lover? I didn't want to think about it.

My mother also told me that Dad's personality change included verbal abuse and cruelty toward her. At one dinner with friends, he poured salt into her coffee cup when she wasn't looking, and she only realized what he had done when she took a sip. Once when he had filled the urinal, he set it on her bed (they still had twin beds under one headboard) so that it fell over and spilled on her sheets and mattress. He blew his nose, finger at one nostril, on her fine bedroom drapes.

Since Mom was almost a decade older than Dad, she became more of a mother than a wife to him, and he rebelled against her in every possible way—a big passive-aggressive rebellion like that of a teenaged boy.

To the world, Dad achieved everything he set out to do and fashioned a new identity for himself from the red clay soil of southwest Virginia. To me and others who loved him, he remained an enigma. He had walled himself off from his family and maybe even from himself.

When I could gain some objectivity, questions came to me. Was Dad bi-polar? Was his depression not treated with medication? Was he offered electroconvulsive therapy like Grandma Sadye and turned it down? Had he abused drugs? How often did he turn to the secret flask of whiskey? I had so many questions with no answers.

The one unassailable fact was that the father I had once loved and admired was gone forever. And I would never know him.

# 44

Three and a half decades after Dad's death, my cousin Joe—the Nazi memorabilia-collecting specter from my childhood—reappeared in my life. Once I left home, I had assiduously avoided him and his older brother, creepy David. Joe was the last surviving member of his family. Uncle Walter died of heart disease in 1986, six years after my father's death, David of a heart attack at age forty-three, and Aunt Martha of a blood cancer at eighty-two—two years before my mother's death. The boy with the swastika flag over his bed was by that time a sixty-two-year-old man.

After Aunt Martha died, Joe held a few odd jobs as a security guard and store cashier and eventually lived on disability in a small trailer home in Dobson, North Carolina. He'd had two major heart attacks and bypass surgery, and his weight and heart condition confined him to a wheelchair. In later years, Mary and Jane visited him annually after Thanksgiving or Christmas. During one of those visits, Mary said Joe brought out a small, clear plastic box and told her that the container held human ashes from Dachau. Joe wanted help in finding a burial place for the remains.

Mary and I phoned each other regularly, and she told me about the task Joe had set for her and what she was doing about it.

She attempted to place the ashes with the Holocaust Memorial Museum in Washington, DC, and other Jewish museums, but all failed. In frustration, she brought the ashes on one of her holiday visits and handed the container over to me. When I looked inside, I saw a misshapen disk of a yellowish white, chalk-like substance, not loose ashes. I wondered, Why are these ashes in such a lump?

"Here," she said. "You do something with it."

I took the box from her, not knowing what to say. I muttered something about doing my best to find a resolution.

In my family, I am the sole keeper of our Jewish heritage. I have all of Grandpa Herman's personal effects, his last passport, his red velvet-covered Jewish prayer book, his prayer shawl (a tallit), as well as every gift he ever brought me from Europe, right down to the red beanie from Switzerland with edelweiss stitched on it. So it made sense that my sister would give the ashes to me. By doing so, she triggered a series of events that brought me closer to Joe.

I discovered that Joe has an encyclopedic knowledge of the world's religions and is an ordained interfaith minister, having acquired his credentials online. His interest in other religions began when he was in his late teens.

"I read *The Egyptian Book of the Dead*, the Quran, the Vedas, the Upanishads, *The Tibetan Book of the Dead*, Confucius, everything I could get my hands on, and I still keep reading," Joe told me in one phone conversation. "Did you know that there was something like the Ten Commandments in *The Egyptian Book of the Dead?* All the original texts of these religions contain the same stories that are in the Old Testament. I see them as stepping-stones to the Bible.

"I tried to talk to my parents about my insights, but they just pushed me off, saying I was talking nonsense," he continued. "I was feeling down then, almost suicidal, when I couldn't pay off a debt to a job agency, and it scared me. My parents said, 'You're lost; you need to talk to the preacher.' So I spoke with the minister. During our meeting, I told him that I'd done a lot of reading about religion and thought it was interesting. I told him that I'd read *The Egyptian Book of the Dead*. The next Sunday, he called me out in front of the whole congregation. Said I was reading a book of the devil. My parents didn't do anything to defend me. They just sat there."

"What a horrible thing to do to someone. You sought his help, and he betrayed you. Fundamentalist fools like him make my blood boil."

"I never went back to that church."

"And who could blame you?"

In talking at length over many phone conversations, I learned that Joe was the real victim of David's physical and sexual abuse.

Joe told me, "Mom knew about David. She even walked in on us when David was sticking his finger up my butt. She acted oblivious. When I told her about all the times David messed with me and that I was scared, she shrugged. Deal with it, she implied. Mom and Dad were afraid of David. He could be violent. As long as he was targeting me, they were spared."

As shocking as Joe's revelations were, I was not surprised. I had feared David, too, and knew he was a predator. I never forgot his leering looks and the time I barely escaped his clutches on our trip to the movies. Sorrow and empathy for Joe welled up in me. I had no idea what he'd endured growing up, and I felt guilty about pushing him out of my life for so long, lumping him in with David.

We would have many phone conversations over the coming months, mostly about the Dachau ashes and what I was doing to find a burial for them.

"I just want these ashes to be buried with dignity," Joe said.

I had countless questions about their origin and how they came to be in Joe's possession. Joe provided the story.

"Dad brought them back from Germany and kept them hidden in a drawer. He never talked about the war the way Uncle Hugh did. I didn't know the ashes existed."

"When did you find out?"

"In the year before Dad died, he brought them out and told me the whole story."

Joe said that in a fit of anger as a teen, he accused his dad of being nothing but a pencil pusher when others were in combat. In fact, Uncle Walter had volunteered for the Army Air Corps, like Dad, but he was disqualified because of an irregular heartbeat and assigned instead to clerical duty.

"When I challenged Dad about his role in the war, he brought out the WWII medals he'd earned and other stuff, including a German cigarette case with something in it," Joe told me. "I asked him what was in the cigarette case, but he started crying and shaking, and Mom told me to shut up. I was upsetting him, and he didn't want to talk about it."

By the time Joe learned the whole story, he was a man approaching middle age, and his father was dying of heart failure. It went thus: Uncle Walter had been sent from Munich, where he was stationed, to Dachau as a messenger just after Germany surrendered in May 1945. He asked to see the concentration camp. A former prisoner showed him around Dachau. Near the ovens, the man scooped up a compressed lump of ashes and handed it to Uncle Walter with the words, "Take this so you will never forget what happened here."

As Joe spoke, I got chills. I was curious about one detail, so I asked, "What did your dad put the ashes in when he was given them at the camp?"

"All he had was his German cigarette case, so he put the ashes in that."

It was a sad irony, I thought, that what were likely Jewish ashes were stored in a German cigarette case.

I asked how the ashes came to be in the clear plastic box, and Joe said that he transferred them to the box for safekeeping. I worried that he'd handled them in the process, but he said no; he shifted the ashes without touching them. Then he put the box in a dresser drawer. For twenty-six years, Joe followed his father's example and kept the ashes hidden.

But there was one question that still haunted me, and after Joe and I had talked several times, I dredged up the courage to ask it.

"Why did you collect Nazi artifacts? I still remember the swastika hanging above your bed."

"I don't know. I just wanted to at the time."

"Didn't you wonder if my dad might be offended by it?"

"Not really."

Joe said this matter-of-factly. He was young then and perhaps didn't understand the full impact of what he was doing at the time. He said what he remembered most about my father was that he was always behind his movie camera, recording the family get-togethers. He said this apologetically.

"I wish I could remember more about your father, but I had such an awful childhood that I blocked out as much as possible."

I asked him, "Why did you hide the ashes for so long after Uncle Walter died, and why bring them out now?"

"I put them away to try and forget about them, because

I didn't know what to do. I brought them out because I was afraid I would die and nobody would know what was in the box and might throw it away."

The enormity of my task and my solemn duty to see it through became clear.

"Thank you for this. It's important," I told Joe. "And I'll make sure these remains are buried with honor and remembrance."

But I procrastinated, not knowing how to begin. For more than a year, the box with the ashes rested in a blown glass bowl on top of my dining room console. The box wasn't visible unless you looked down into the bowl.

I began to understand Joe's reluctance to deal with the ashes. Though the ashes were sitting in the middle of my house, I avoided thinking about them. I believed there were human remains in that box, so I numbed myself to it for months, trying to forget it was there.

I feared that Joe would die without having closure, so I finally began making inquiries, which ultimately led me to Sharon Halperin, the daughter of two holocaust survivors and co-founder of the local Holocaust Speaker's Bureau. In a halting voice, I told Sharon my account over the phone and asked for her help.

"This is an amazing story, and I want to meet you and see the ashes," Sharon said.

It was a huge relief that someone with Sharon's *bona fides* would be seriously interested in what I had to say. I had been worried that those ashes would stay with me and be on my conscience forever.

We arranged to meet at a Chapel Hill coffee shop the following week.

When the day arrived, I was both anxious and hopeful. That small, light box was a weight so heavy, I feared I couldn't bear up under it if Sharon didn't help me shoulder the burden. The ashes, what was left of real people, had been waiting nearly seven decades to be acknowledged.

We had described ourselves on the phone, so when I walked in on a late fall afternoon, it was easy to spot Sharon among the tables crowded with young people in sweatshirts and hoodies, working on their laptops, listening to their headphones. Sharon was a slim blonde with a lovely, warm face and was wearing an orange jacket. She waved to me when I entered the door.

Together, we went to the counter, ordered our beverages, and took our drinks back to the table.

I slid into the chair opposite her, placing a small paper bag with handles on the table between us. I had put the ashes in the bag to protect them and keep the box upright.

"I hope you can help me," I said, trying to keep the pleading tone out of my voice.

Sharon smiled encouragingly.

"Tell me again about these ashes and how you came to have them."

I took a sip of tea and recounted to Sharon the story of the ashes as Joe told it to me.

"But how do you know they're authentic?" Sharon asked. With this question, I wilted a little.

"I don't know. I only know what my cousin told me, which his father related to him."

"May I see them?"

"Yes, of course," I said, as I pulled the plastic container from the paper bag and handed it to Sharon. Loud pop music I didn't recognize was playing on the coffee shop's speakers. Bringing out ashes from a Nazi death camp to banal lyrics banging from the speakers was incongruous and surreal.

Sharon's eyes widened as she took the box from my fingers. "Oh, my God," she exclaimed as she opened the box and looked at the chalky contents. "I can't believe this is really happening." She looked at me as if seeing me for the first time.

"I know." I took a deep breath. "It's strange—how these ashes came to me."

Having the ashes was a stark reminder that had I lived in Nazi-occupied Europe, I would have been considered a Jew and treated accordingly. Grandpa Herman only just escaped the Nazis when he left Vienna where he'd been studying with composer Leopold Godowski.

I had told Sharon something of my background, as if to prove my legitimacy, my right to be there with her. I needed her to know that I was 50 percent Jew.

"We can't do anything about this until we can confirm that the ashes are human and date to WWII."

"But how do we accomplish that?" My voice caught as I anticipated a letdown.

"As it happens, my husband is chancellor of New York Medical College and has connections with the New York City medical examiner's office—the one that identified remains from 9/11. May I take these remains and give them to Ed?"

"Absolutely."

Sharon gently put the container with its precious contents back in the bag, and we said our goodbyes. The ashes were safe and in the right hands. For the first time, I could rest easier. There was the question of whether the ashes were authentic, but I had no doubt that they were.

"I'll call you as soon as I find out something," she said.

As promised, Dr. Ed Halperin carried the ashes to the NYC medical examiner's office for analysis. The findings were that the ashes contained collagen, protein, and hemoglobin. They were human remains.

The lab identified the compressed ashes as an ash-cake. I learned that early in WWII, in an attempt to disguise what they were doing in the death camps, the

Nazis sometimes compacted ashes into cakes that were stamped with a number. They did this to have something to give to relatives, claiming their loved ones died of natural causes, rather than being murdered in the camps. It didn't matter to them that cremation was abhorrent to Jews.

The ashcakes the Nazis manufactured contained a mix of different human remains, though they portrayed the ashcakes as the remains of one Jewish family member. The Nazis used the ashcakes as a public relations ploy to deflect suspicion that they were executing people in the camps. The partial cake I had from Joe showed only a fragmented faint outline of what had once been numbers.

Sharon, who, I was soon to discover, was a get-it-done woman, formed a committee, including two local rabbis and me, to plan a service and burial in Durham's Hebrew cemetery. Under Jewish law, cremation of a dead body is considered a desecration and is forbidden. The law doesn't apply to those who were cremated against their will. That's why the ashcake could be buried with full rites in the Hebrew cemetery.

We met regularly for a few months to map out the logistics and the service. I had been living in Durham for years and had seen the Hebrew cemetery, belonging to Beth El Synagogue, with the small rocks resting atop its gravestones, long a Jewish tradition denoting permanence and remembrance. Being included in planning the ceremony felt good and right. It harkened back to my strong ties to my Jewish grandparents. I never forget that I'm a half-Jew and proud of it.

Thanks to Sharon and her connections, *The New York Times* ran an article on Joe and the ashcake in its religion section, titled, "A Resolution at Last for a Father's Unsettling Legacy." A *Times* reporter traveled to Dobson to interview Joe for the story, which included a current photo of Joe, one of a young Uncle Walter in his WWII uniform, and the ashcake. My sister and I were mentioned in the article. A couple of my Jewish friends and a second cousin on my Jewish side contacted me to thank me for what I'd done. I felt the gratitude should go to others. I was just the intermediary.

In May of 2014, we held the ceremony in a special location at the cemetery. Mary drove down from Washington. Durham's mayor came, along with television and print media. One of my jobs on the committee had been to write a press release and send it to media outlets and then follow up.

Many holocaust survivors were there in short sleeves, the numbers tattooed on their arms still visible. Thanks to the kindness of a stranger who offered to drive him, Joe was able to make the 120-mile trip from Dobson to attend the ceremony. There he was, under the funeral tent, in a wheelchair, wearing his clerical robes for the first time in public. Sharon and each of the two rabbis, one female and one male, made their remarks.

I felt the weight of my split history and my divided loyalties. I wanted to belong to this tribe, but at the same time I felt like an imposter. Dad had abandoned Judaism and my mother was a Gentile. In my quest to find a place where I belonged, I had attended synagogue when I was a young woman, but I didn't feel the call to worship with Jews any more than I did with Gentiles.

Since Joe couldn't walk or be wheeled to the gravesite, he remained under the tent. Sharon and the rabbis gave me the honor of carrying the ashcake in a special wooden box—made for the occasion with a Star of David carved on the top—to the gravesite. I walked slowly and solemnly to the place where two members of the synagogue were waiting to take the box and lower it on ropes

*The author carrying the small wooden box containing ashes from Dachau to its burial place.*

into a shallow grave. On the short walk to the grave, grief pounded like a fist inside me, although I didn't cry. Tears were insufficient to mourn such tragedy.

After the box was seated in its grave, a line formed of those who wished to throw dirt on the tiny casket. Holocaust survivors were at the front of the line—and I, the interloper. As each person filed past, some bent and others with canes, I heard one and then another say, as they tossed dirt into the grave, "For my mother. For my sister. For my husband. For my wife. For my brother."

As my turn came, I grabbed a handful of dirt, dropped it into the grave, and whispered, "For my grandfather, for my father."

❖❖❖❖❖

*Therefore, the Master of Mercy will protect him forever, from behind the hiding of his wings, and will tie his soul with the rope of life. The Everlasting is his heritage, and he shall rest peacefully upon his lying place, and let us say: Amen.*

— JEWISH PRAYER FOR THE DEAD

# ❦❦❦❦ AFTERWORD ❦❦❦❦

I have been writing this memoir for twenty years, beginning after my mother died in 2000. A sibling's pushback, after an essay on my father's death was published in a book of women's writing, shut me down for years. But the memoir was still percolating inside me. Late in 2017, I had dinner with a supportive and loving friend. I told her that an insistent voice in my head was pushing me to write the memoir. I said, through tears, that I thought I would perish if I didn't write this book.

She said, "Write it."

I had been swimming against the current with my old comrade, depression. Writing was a life raft. And so I began pulling out dusty files containing essays about my childhood and my life as an adult. I started writing and didn't stop, even when I felt stuck or suspicious about my memories. I was driven to write. As I wrote, more memories surfaced, including dialog that I knew to be true.

My goal was to understand my father, why he was sometimes cruel, what drove him to suicide. Did he love me? Who was he?

I didn't find answers to those questions. Instead, I learned things about myself that years of psychotherapy, though important, had not revealed. The seeds of my lifelong depression had been planted early, and it was probably also in my DNA. Feeling unworthy and not good enough was inherited from parents who had doubts about their own worth. If you're treated as though you are not worthy, you spend a lifetime trying to prove it. Fundamentalism perpetuated the myth of unworthiness.

Being the firstborn does not mean always being cherished. Through no fault of your own, you can be sidelined in favor of younger siblings who need more attention. After my brother was born, what I thought was my secure bond with my father broke irrevocably.

That broken bond led to searching for the same unreachable qualities in other men and trying to make the outcome different. It never worked. It led to bad choices.

Readers will not be surprised to know that Will and I parted ways when our sons were still young. I was gutted and riven with guilt at subjecting my sons to the life of vagabonds moving between two houses every other week. I spent the next fifteen years as a guilty part-time single parent and more years alone after my sons left for college. I worked hard as a writer and communications director. I had some fleeting relationships. Fundamentally, I was lonely—a familiar feeling and one I could live with.

I felt most alive when traveling, often alone, to new places. Travel was my salvation from a world of routine and sometimes thankless work. Every year, at least once, I travelled abroad—from Europe to South America to Tahiti and to Japan a second time. And yes, I went to Paris more times than I can count, and I fell in love with it.

I had bouts of depression along the way, sometimes with thoughts of suicide. Not wanting to put my sons through what I suffered with my father kept me going when every fiber of my being wanted to give up and sleep forever, to be relieved of the torment I carried. Back pain and other limiting physical pain had changed my life, too, but I learned that I had the strength that my father lacked to stay alive. And not only to stay alive, but to prosper.

I've been a life-long learner, always investigating new information, learning new skills, nourishing my creative life. After more than twenty years as a single woman, I met and married a new life partner who is able to support my explorations and relate to my feelings. Now, I know that I'm living my best life, with a loving husband, two beautiful grandchildren, good friends, creative work and play, and reveling in the natural world, still my cathedral.

The best outcome is that I am at last rid of debilitating depression. Perhaps aging had something to do with it. Perhaps writing this book helped. Whatever the reason, I will not miss my old energy-sapping companion.

〜〜〜〜 ACKNOWLEDGMENTS 〜〜〜〜

This book would have been impossible without the love, guidance, support, and wisdom of many people, most especially my talented writing group, led by author and teacher, the inestimable Nancy Peacock. You pushed me to go farther and deeper than I would have known possible. Your continuing support and encouragement buoyed me when my wheels got stuck. Thank you Lisa Bobst, Denise Cline, Linda Janssen, Sara Johnson, and Ann Parrent.

To my readers, of both the early drafts and the later ones, I owe you. Anastasia Toufexis, longtime friend, editor, and writer, provided critical feedback in the beginning and stuck by me throughout. Author and writing teacher Virginia Holman read an early and not terribly good first draft. She dropped the hammer on me gently. Author Lee Smith took an interest in my book and gave me a boost just when I needed it.

Readers (and writers all) Joan Barasovska, Judith Ernst, Sara Johnson, Anne Moore, and Carolyn Schwartz—you are dear to me and gave me insight. Likewise, I thank Bill Schwartz and Hy Muss. Your enthusiasm is infectious.

I would be remiss if I did not also thank my cousin, Joe Corsbie, who provided much of the background for the last chapter and tried to help me remember what my father was like when our family visited his. My gratitude also goes to my youngest sister for providing some of the photos you see in the book.

To my husband, Vic Benedict, who read every draft: You are my cheerleader and my rock. I'm so lucky we found each other.

Finally, gratitude and kudos go to Nora Gaskin of Lystra Books and Literary Services. Nora helped shape the final draft with an insightful and spot-on content edit. As a writer, editor, and publisher, Nora has been supportive and wise in all things to do with getting a book to print. Kelly Lojk was a scrupulous copy editor and talented designer who, along with Nora, made up the A-team that got me to the finish line.

I'm grateful to have such accomplished, interesting, and caring people in my life.

CPSIA information can be obtained
at www.ICGtesting.com
Printed in the USA
LVHW032256251120
672678LV00007B/1448